VšĮ ANTANO SUTKAUS
fotografijų archyvas

CULTURAL
DIALOGUE
LTD (UK)

HERALD
of EUROPE
magazine of culture & politics

LIETUVOS
KULTŪROS
TARYBA

LEWBEN | FOUNDARTTION

ISBN 978-0-9557394-9-1

ANTANAS SUTKUS

IN MEMORIAM. TO VILNIUS AND KAUNAS GHETTO PRISONERS

23 September - 22 October 2016

White Space Gallery in partnership with Cultural Dialogue Ltd (UK)
6 Pall Mall East, London SW1Y 5BF

Author's note:

This book could not have been published without the generous help and advice of Antanas and Rima Sutkus, Prof. Michael Borshchevsky, Kamilė Rupeikaitė, Prof. Irena Veisaite, Catherine Harley, Irina Filonova, Petr Favorov, Arturas Morozovas, Leslie and Hugh Reynolds, Nina and Claude Gruen, Sergey Livnev.

Antanas Sutkus wishes to thank the Lithuanian Jewish Community for their support.

ANTANAS SUTKUS

IN MEMORIAM

Vilniaus ir Kauno geto kaliniams

To Vilnius and Kaunas Ghetto Prisoners

white
space
gallery

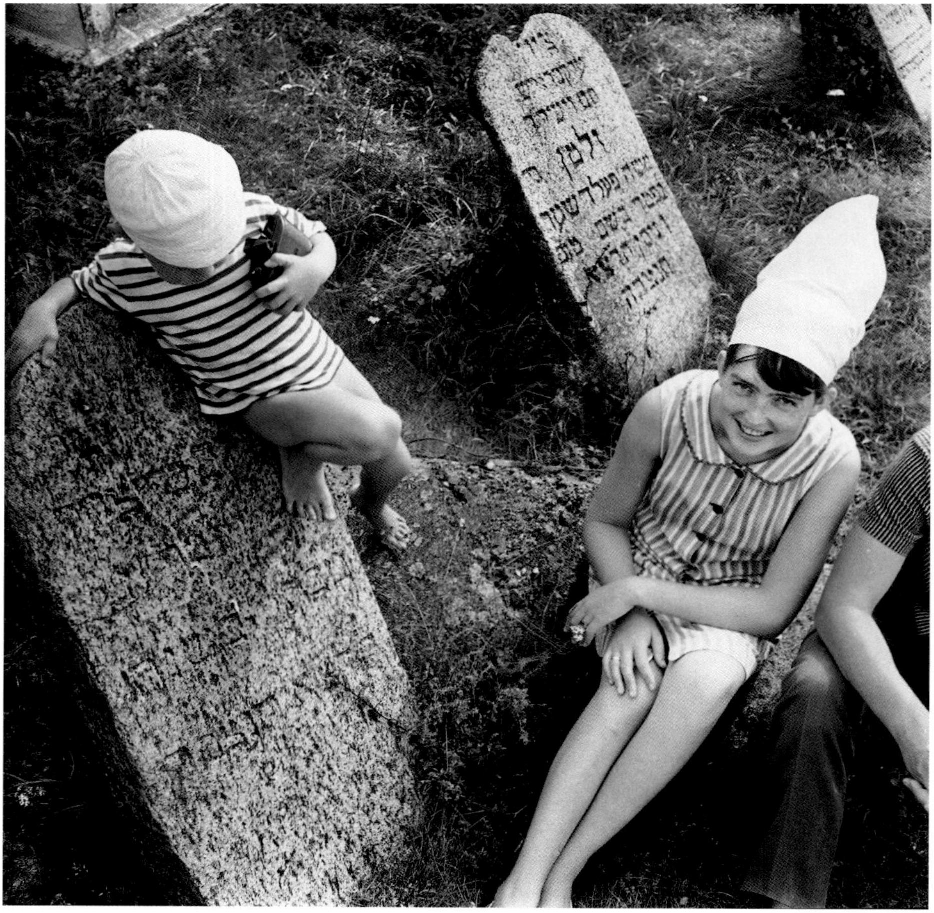

In the Old Jewish Cemetery. Zarasai, 1968

IF I FORGET THEE

The destructive powers of modernity would be unthinkable without forgetting the past, a crucial aspect of modernity's obsessive belief in the future. That dying individuals lose their past rather than the present and the future we learn from the unbearably light and ironic Milan Kuncera and from the tragically prophetic George Orwell as well.

Nonetheless, the politics of remembering is not the way out of the uncertainties and painful dilemmas of modernity. It works as a remedy from the malaise of forgetting and insensitivity as long as it serves as a framework for a dissenting thought. The established politics of remembering begins in a prescriptive mode of self-comprehension; small wonder then that it can turn into a dangerous fixation on selected series of events and historical personalities that would result in the total denial of those individuals and groups that remember in a different fashion.

In fact, remembering reveals the past as a critical aspect of our experience, as something, without which we could never sustain our sensibilities. Yet, when it becomes the axis of political life, we can slide into the tyranny of a frozen time that divides the world into 'us' and 'them'. In doing so, we are at the risk of adopting the Manichaean moral logic that does not allow us to grasp reality as consisting of flesh-and-blood human beings able to change their views, convictions and stances. The tyranny of the past would never allow us to reconcile ourselves with the world, especially when peace with the former political foe and oppressor is at issue.

Yet, if human beings were able to remember everything, they would become totally self-contained and self-sufficient, and, in effect, would end up with dramatically diminished powers of association. Modernity is obsessed with controlling memory and rewriting history in accordance with power distribution or disposition. I am in control of societal existence and culture; therefore, I am able to provide a legitimizing narrative. Memory is an aspect of power. What and how to remember and what and how to forget, depends on who writes an account of an epoch's history and political deeds. Therefore, it makes no sense to confuse the memory of eyewitnesses with the politics of memory established by states to justify their deeds and, most importantly, to legitimize their present policies.

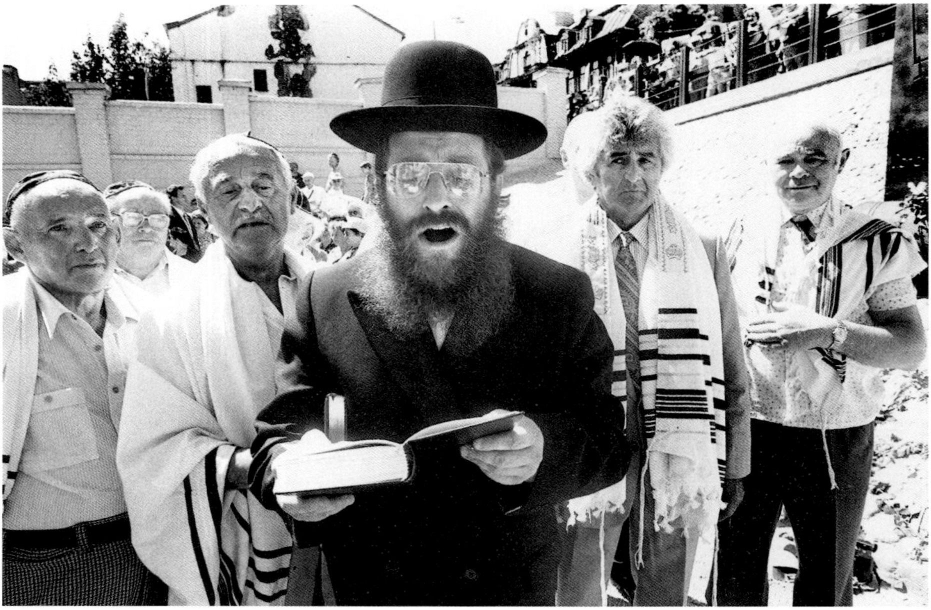

Commemoration meeting to mark the 50th anniversary of the liquidation of the Kaunas ghetto. Prayers at the monument to the killed children. 1994

Whatever the case, we are bound to answer the existential questions: should we memorize and keep everything for the generations to come, prolonging the existence of and giving a second life to those who deserve it? I remember, therefore I am? To forget what is irrational and does not qualify for the realm of collective memory? These are two opposed, if not mutually exclusive, promises of modernity.

History and culture appears as a meaningful and silent moral alternative to the brutality of power politics carried out by the powerful. Memory becomes a tool of the small and weak, while forgetting best serves the interests of the big and mighty. In this way, memory manifests itself as an alternative moral imagination in opposition to the logic of power. Memory uncovers the essence of that logic of power, as a conscious effort to continue or prolong the existence of what deserves to exist.

The Holocaust continues to be the most tragic event in human history. Not because we are necessarily facing the inevitable new holocausts, which we can never exclude as at least a remote possibility, but due to the sad fact that very few Holocaust survivors are around. Their faces, eyes, looks and hands retreat along with their life and death stories, the nightmares of betrayal and brutality they experienced, and the miracles of humanity they witnessed.

Human life is vulnerable and fragile, yet so is our ability to remember the tragedies of humanity. With the passing of the last survivors, we will face a tough ordeal as to how to think about the unthinkable, and how to speak about the unspeakable? How to do it when the living testimony of the major crime of human history is withering and vanishing before our eyes?

Therefore, culture can become a mode of humanity's existential memory. Great artists depicting, portraying or else individualizing their contemporaries become part of the process of a conscious continuation of someone else's existence.

This is exactly what Antanas Sutkus, a humanist Lithuanian photographer, the master of candid photography and of the portrait of an unknown person, tries to achieve with his exhibition Pro Memoria devoted to the memory of the Holocaust in Lithuania. The theme of the Holocaust is pivotal, as Lithuania is a country of the tragic past: during the Second World War, the country, which was home for the largest Jewish community in the Baltic region, the community famous for its creativity and achievements in culture all over Europe, lost that community nearly entirely. The facts can tell us something about the scale of the tragedy: that around 240,000 Lithuanian Jews perished during the Holocaust, and that only 20,000 survived it, is the astonishing and awful statistics.

Yet, we need a living testimony: the faces, eyes and hands of survivors who will not allow us to forget the crime against humanity. To reconcile ourselves with our past and history, we need the Face, rather than numbers.

In this, Antanas Sutkus becomes our guide into the world of memory enacted through the eyes of the survivor: his camera, with the flash of genius, becomes a continuation of existence, as if to say that life will go on as long as we can establish an eye-to-eye and a face-to-face relationship.

For there are things that can never be forgotten. If I forget thee, whose face and eyes I saw, then woe to me, since I had abandoned humanity.

Leonidas Donskis
Professor of Politics at Vytautas Magnus University,
Kaunas, Lithuania

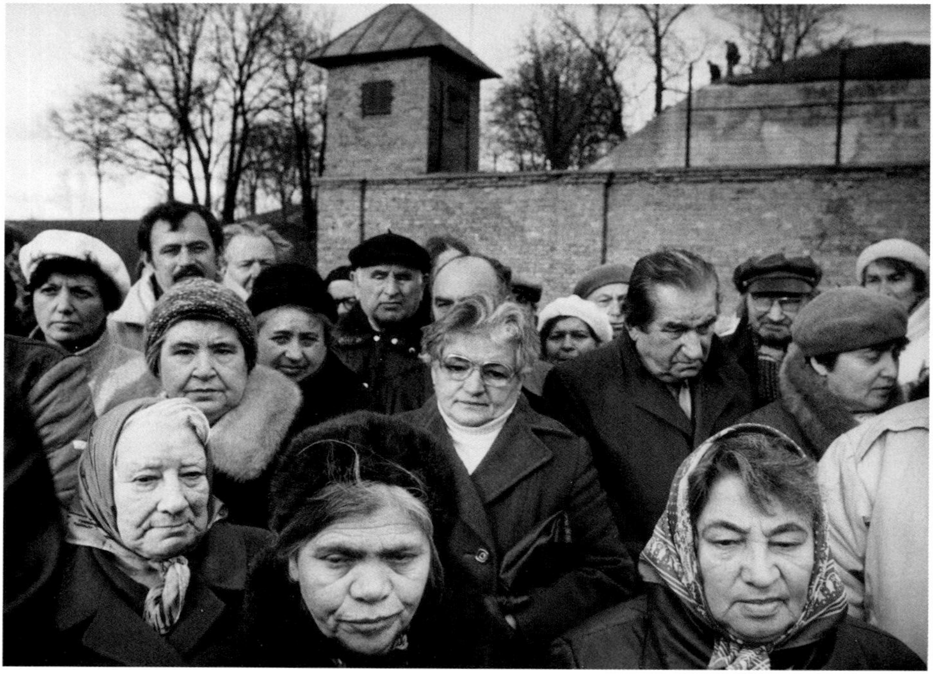

The unsanctioned meeting at the Kaunas 9th fort – the place of the mass killing of Jews. 1988

KAUNAS GHETTO

Jews began settling in Kaunas in the second half of the 17th century. They were not allowed to live in the city, so most of them stayed in the **Vilijampolė** (known to Jews as Slobodka) settlement on the right bank of the river Neris.

The Jewish population of Kaunas began to grow in the early decades of the 19th century; before the WWII, it reached nearly 33,000 (about thirty percent of the town's population). After all residential and occupational restrictions on Jews in Kaunas were lifted in the second half of the 19th century, the city began to emerge as a major centre of Jewish culture, enterprise, and scholarship. Slobodka Yeshiva, founded in 1882, was one of the biggest and most known in Europe. Between the world wars, there were more than thirty synagogues, a large number of Yiddish schools, four Hebrew high schools, a Jewish hospital, and five Jewish daily newspapers in Kaunas.

After Lithuania declared its independence in 1918, the situation was tough as Soviet Russia started an invasion at the end of the year. Jews were active participants and supporters of the Lithuanian independence. A national cultural, religious, social, and educational autonomy, granted to the Jewish community, was a unique example in the history of rights of ethnic minorities. It was done due to the country's need for the support of Jews in the initial stage of gaining its independence. When the hard-line nationalists came to power in 1926, random cases of intolerance towards Jews happened; however, the government condemned such cases and fought against it. From 1934, acceptances of Jewish students into the Vytautas Magnus University decreased significantly; Jews were driven out of the economy, a number of negative articles were published by the Lithuanian press.

Jewish life in Kaunas was unsettled when the Soviet Union occupied Lithuania in June 1940, remaining there until June 22nd 1941, up until the German invasion. From June 23rd 1941, Kaunas was controlled by the White Armbands of the Lithuanian Activists Front (LAF), who arrested Jews on suspicion of collaborating with the Soviet authorities. Two days later, on June 25th when the city came under control of the Nazi army and security police, the persecution of Jews as a nation, not just communists, began. Pogroms were the evidence. The solution to the "Jewish problem" was in the hands of the Nazi security police and the SD Operative Groups and Units. In Kaunas, Unit 1b (Sonderkommando 1b) of the Operative Group A headed by the SS Obersturmbanführer Erich Ehrlinger was in operation. Franz Walter Stahlecker, the chief of the Operative Group A was under the orders to organise Jewish pogroms and killings, and to secure local residents' support. He succeeded in arranging part of the armed pogroms carried out by the Lithuanians. The first pogrom led by Algirdas J. Klimaitis took place at night, on June 26th. The largest pogroms took place in **Vilijampolė**. Attacks by the White Armbands armed with guns, axes, and sticks started on June 25th and went on until June 27th. Over 1,500 Jews were killed, several synagogues were set on fire and about 60 Jewish houses were burnt down. The Jews were beaten, sadistically humiliated in front of their families and then killed inside their houses and on the streets. Kaunas' rabbi Ephraim Oshry, who saw the pogrom, described the events as "the horror unseen by the world". The killings also took place in the centre of the city. One such massacre, particularly vicious, was a killing of the Jewish men in the **Lietūkis** garage in Kaunas on June 27th 1941. Local civilians in the centre of the city killed from fifty to sixty Jews with crowbars, after brutally torturing them. This was witnessed by a crowd of citizens and photographed by German troops in broad daylight.

After pogroms were incited by the Nazis, from July 1941, the systematic killings of Jews at the forts in Kaunas began[1]. The First and Third companies of the TDA (National Labour Defence) battalion, as well as Gestapo men took part in the killings. The VII Fort was the first site, where the mass killings of the Jews started (end of June – beginning of July1941); there were over 3,000 victims. After the establishment of the Kaunas ghetto, the IV Fort served as a killing site (August – September 1941) and from September 26th 1941, massacres only took place in the IX Fort[2]. On October 4th 1941, 1,845 Jews (including 818 children) were killed there. They were the inmates of the Small ghetto the Germans liquidated. The largest massacre, not only at the IX Fort, but in all of Lithuania – the "Great Action" – took place on October 29th 1941.

---

1 Constructed at the end of the 19th century in order to defend tsarist Kaunas from possible enemies, the nine forts surrounded the city. After World War I, they lost their strategic importance and were abandoned. Later the forts were used by the army of the Lithuanian Republic that was being formed, and also served various public purposes. For instance, in the interwar period the IX Fort served as a prison.

2 The special commission for investigating and research of crimes committed by the German Nazis was formed in August 1944. It established that about 50,000 people were killed at the IX Fort; most of them were Lithuanian Jews; about 10,000 Jews were brought from Austria, Germany and France. Some historians maintain that the figure was lower.

The day before, on October 28th, the entire ghetto population was ordered by the German authorities to gather in **Demokratų Square** in the Kaunas ghetto. The square was surrounded by Lithuanian, German and Ukrainian armed units of the auxiliary police battalions. The SS-Hauptscharführer Helmut Rauca performed the selection – "Life or Death" – with one wave of the hand, to the left or to the right. People sent to "The Right" were shot at the IX Fort on October 29th. These were "redundant" 9,200 Jewish men, women and children – about one third of the Kaunas Jewish community...

On July 10th 1941, Kaunas commandant Jurgis Bobelis and city burgomaster **Kazys Palčiauskas**, in response to the decree of Kaunas Commissar Lentzen issued an order, stating that the Jews had to move to the ghetto in **Vilijampolė** until August 15th. From July 12th 1941, all city Jews were to wear a yellow Star of David (8–10 cm in diameter) on the left side of the breast. From July 28th, the Jews were forbidden to walk in the streets, parks and squares and also to use public transport. By August 1st 1941, about ninty percent of the city's Jews had been moved to the ghetto. Fritz Jordan was appointed a commanding officer. By August 15th 1941, the setting up of the Kaunas ghetto had been completed and the first "actions" started. On August 18th, the City Commandant established the Council of Elders (Ältestenrat). Dr. Elchanan Elkes was elected the chairman (Oberjude). The council was responsible for communicating with the Germans on administrative matters. Together with the police, the Council of Elders was to keep order in the ghetto of about 30,000 people (before the war, about 6,000 people lived in that area). Every day the council members had to tackle difficult problems: how to protect the people from starvation, disease and the constant threat of death. The council, with meagre resources, was responsible for seventeen offices. The ghetto police was established to keep up order. Much attention was paid to the prevention of contagious diseases; there was a hospital with qualified physicians and a sanitary service. About 9,000 able-bodied Jews were imprisoned in the ghetto; working meant an opportunity for them to stay alive for some time longer. The Council of Elders paid much attention to the labour force and labour productivity, taking efforts to have as many workers and work enterprises as possible. Numerous ghetto workshops were of great importance: a tailor, a bakery, a shoemaker, a laundry, toy workshops, tinsmiths, saddle makers and others. Women worked in the vegetable fields; many shift work teams went to work outside the ghetto. The Council of Elders supported every initiative to boost the people's morality whenever it

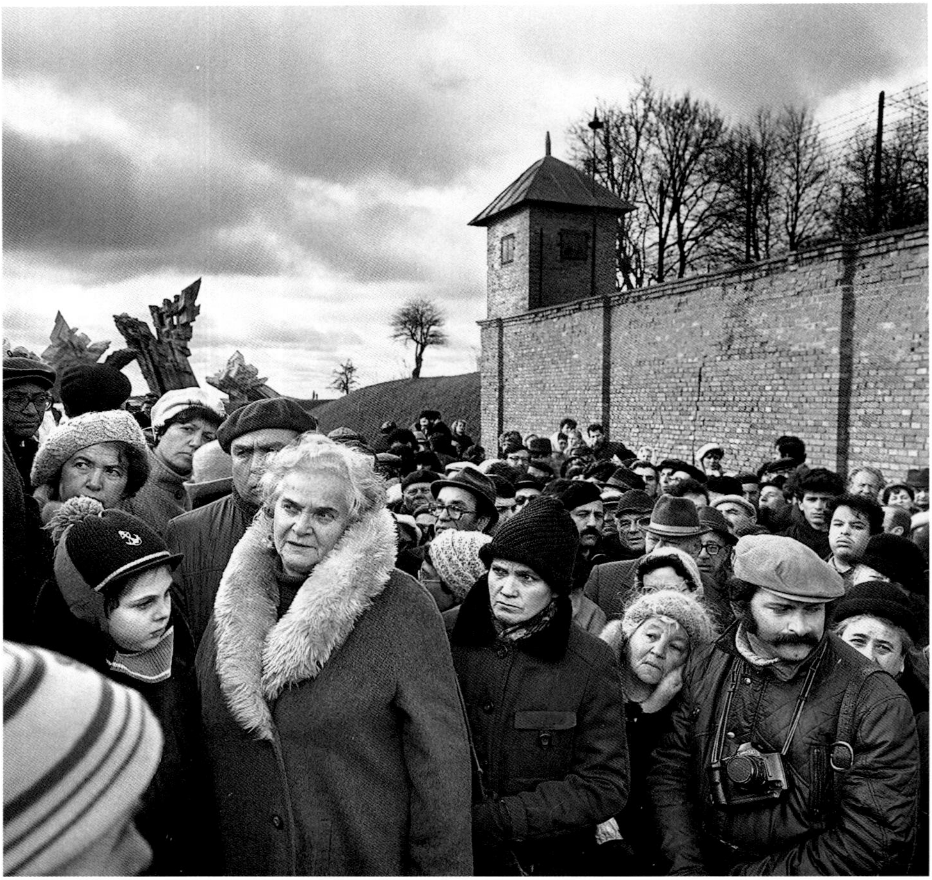

The unsanctioned meeting at the Kaunas 9th fort – the place of the mass killing of Jews. 1988

was possible: teach the children, help the poor, organise meetings, stage performances, hold concerts. A school was opened, at times a kindergarten operated, a children's choir was formed; there were several clubs and a ballet studio. In the middle of 1942, the ghetto musicians formed a police orchestra (as quite a number of musicians worked for the ghetto police), led by a famous violin virtuoso and conductor Michael Hofmekler. Before the war, he was the leader of Hofmekler Brothers Ensemble and Metropolis' orchestra. The first symphonic orchestra concert took place in August 1942, at the Slobodka Yeshiva. There were other artists and poets in the ghetto. Participation in cultural events was the only escape from the terrible reality people had for a short time.

At the end of 1941, underground Communist and Zionist resistance organisations were in operation; on the initiative of Haim Yellin they were joined into the Anti-fascist Fight Organisation (AKO). They bolstered a membership of 500, and Yellin was elected its leader. The organisation's goal was an active armed resistance against the Nazis; another goal was to lead as many of its members to Soviet partisans as was possible.

At the beginning of October 1943, the Kaunas ghetto was turned into concentration camp KL-Kauen. Its civilian authorities were replaced by the SS. Wilhelm Göcke, the SS-Obersturmbanführer, who was appointed commandant of the camp. The control of the ghetto became stricter – the ghetto self-government was abolished and amateur activities were forbidden. With the Nazi positions weakening at the front, in November 1943, a team was formed to exhume and burn the dead at IX Fort. This was in order to hide the scope of Nazi crimes. It consisted of 64 prisoners – ghetto Jews and POWs. They escaped on November 25th 1943 realising what awaited them if they would finish that work.

On March 27-28th 1944, the Gestapo aided by Ukrainian and Vlasov troops carried out the extremely atrocious "Children action" at KL-Kauen, where children under the age of 12 were separated from their mothers, thrown into trucks and taken away. Adults over 55 and disabled persons were also the target of this "action". After two days of hunt, more than 1,000 people were taken to Auschwitz, and approximately 300 were shot at the IX Fort.

On July 8–12th 1944, the ghetto was liquidated and the houses were set on fire. Some 6,000 to 7,000 Jews were taken to Dachau and Stutthof concentration camps; about 1,000 were killed when the ghetto had been liquidated; about 300 or 400 Jews managed to escape. On August 1st 1944, the Red Army entered Kaunas.

Neringa Latvytė-Gustaitienė, Kamilė Rupeikaitė

Vilna Gaon State Jewish Museum

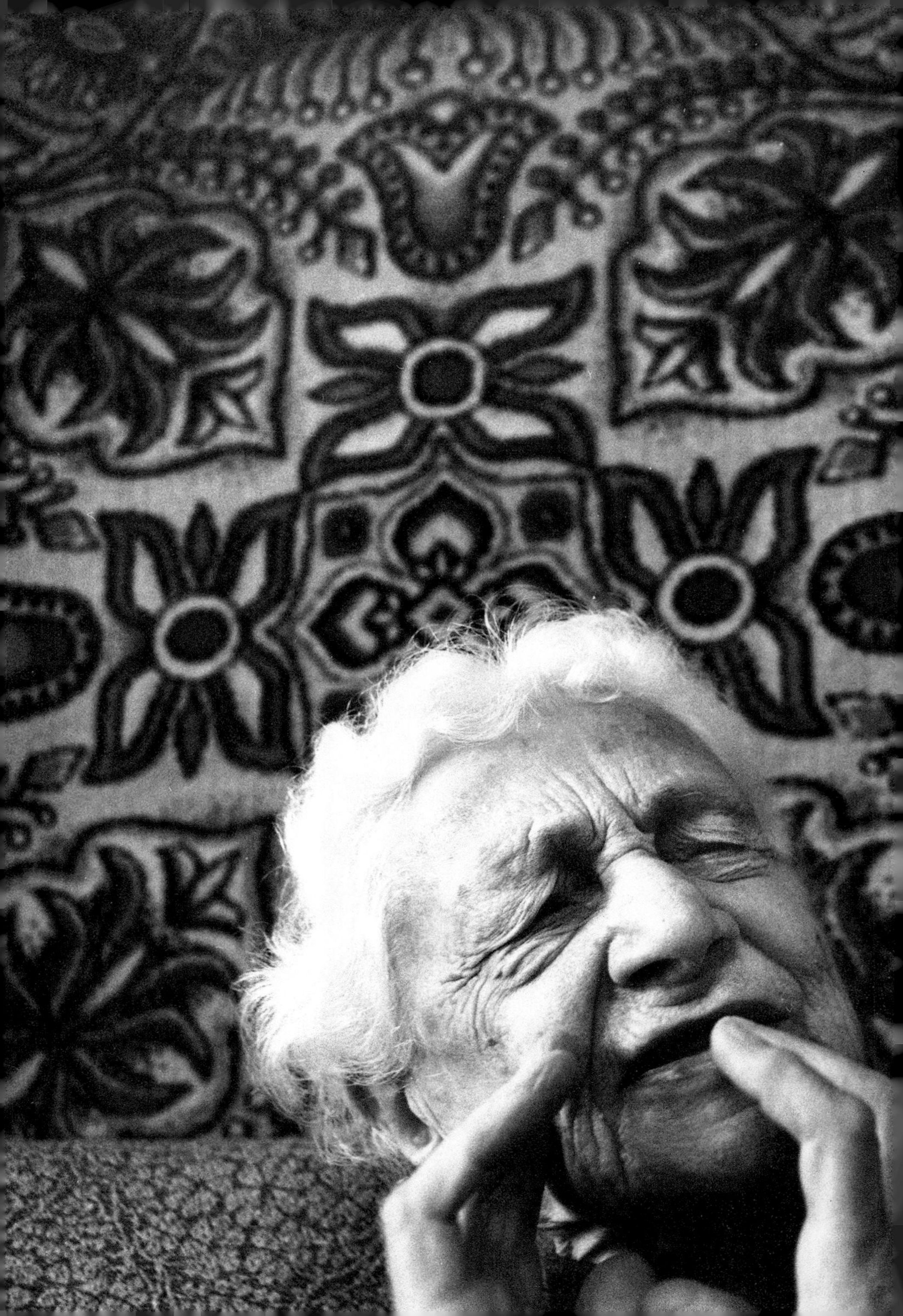

ANTANAS SUTKUS

Portraits 1988-1997

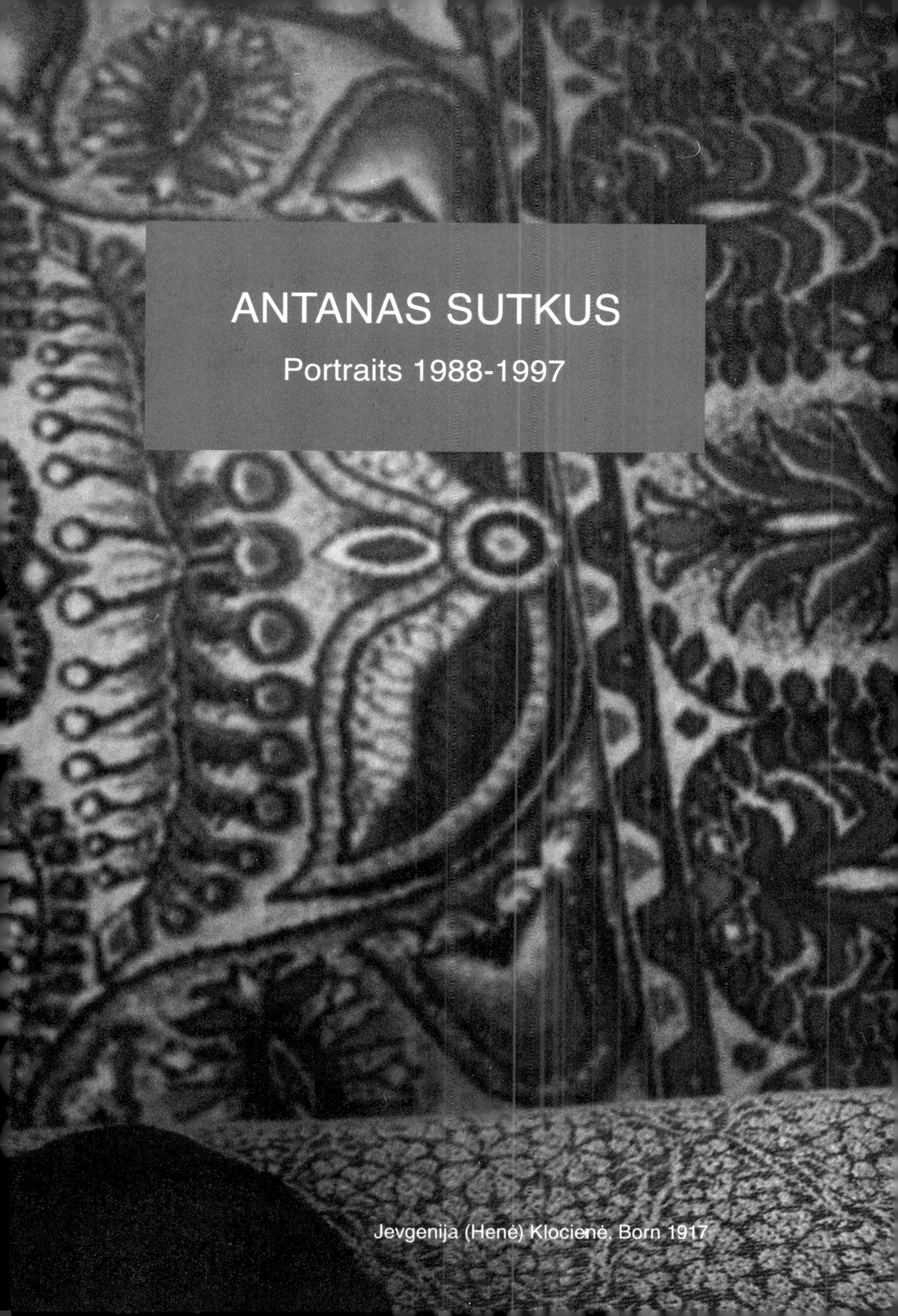

Jevgenija (Henė) Klocienė, Born 1917

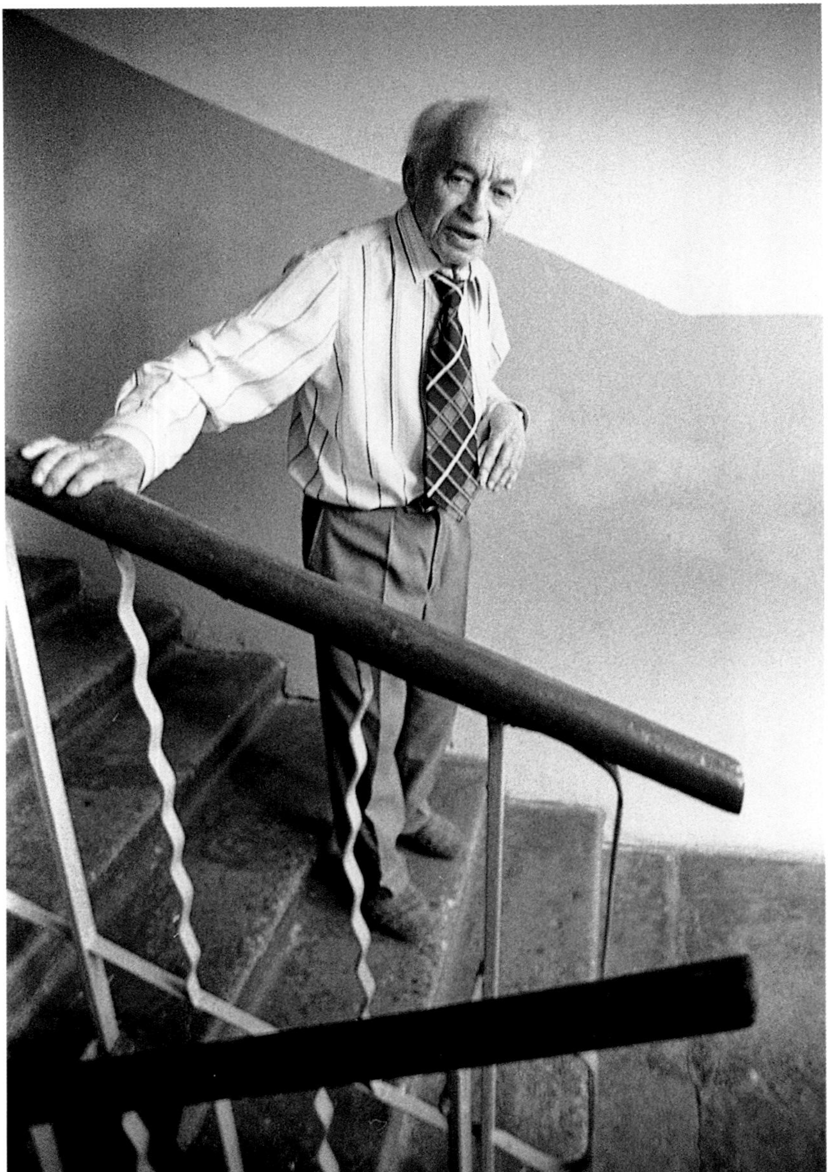

Dovydas Glikas. Born 1911

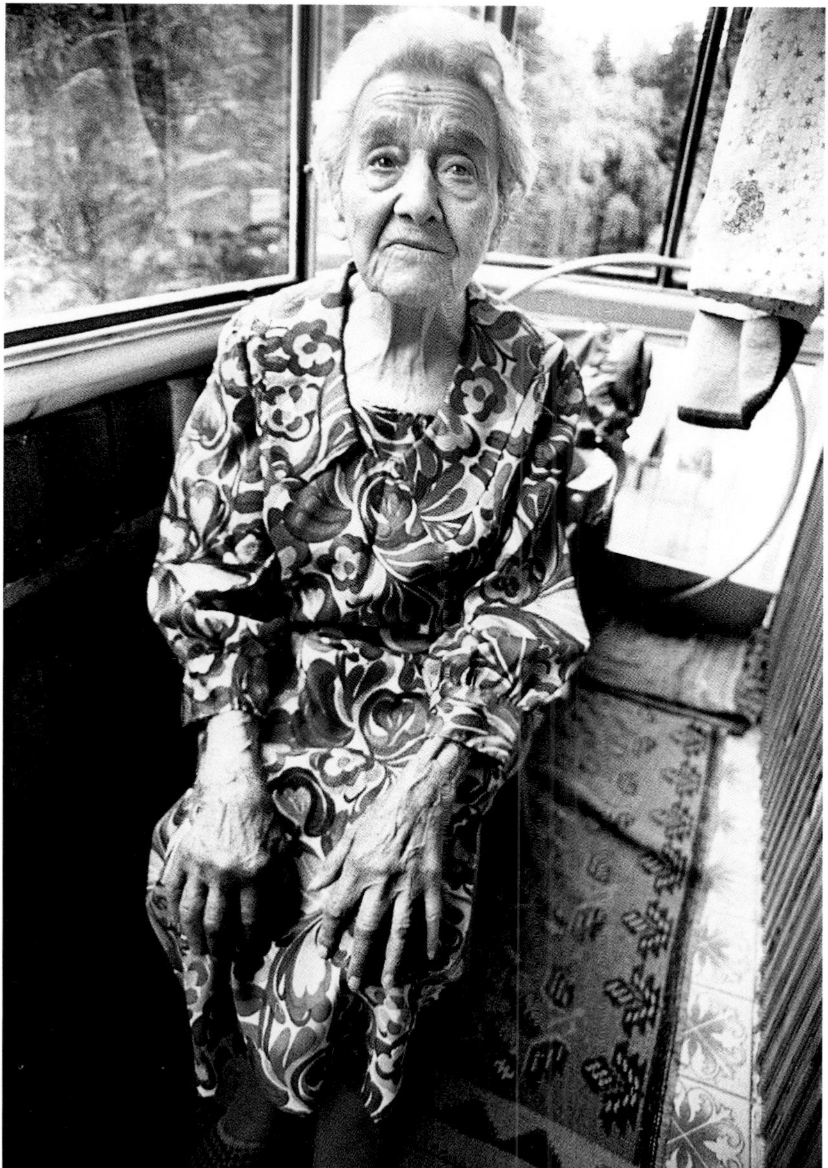

Chaja Korbienė. Born 1909

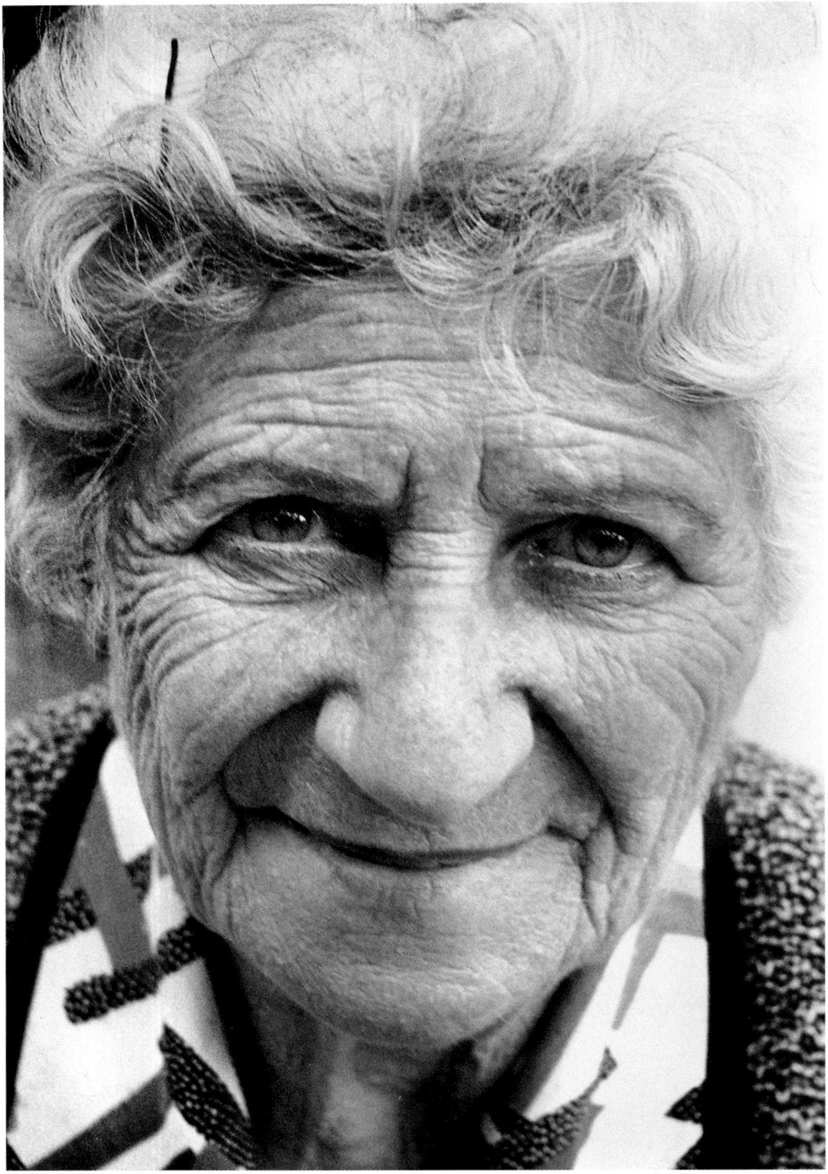

Basia Zagorskienė. Born. 1922

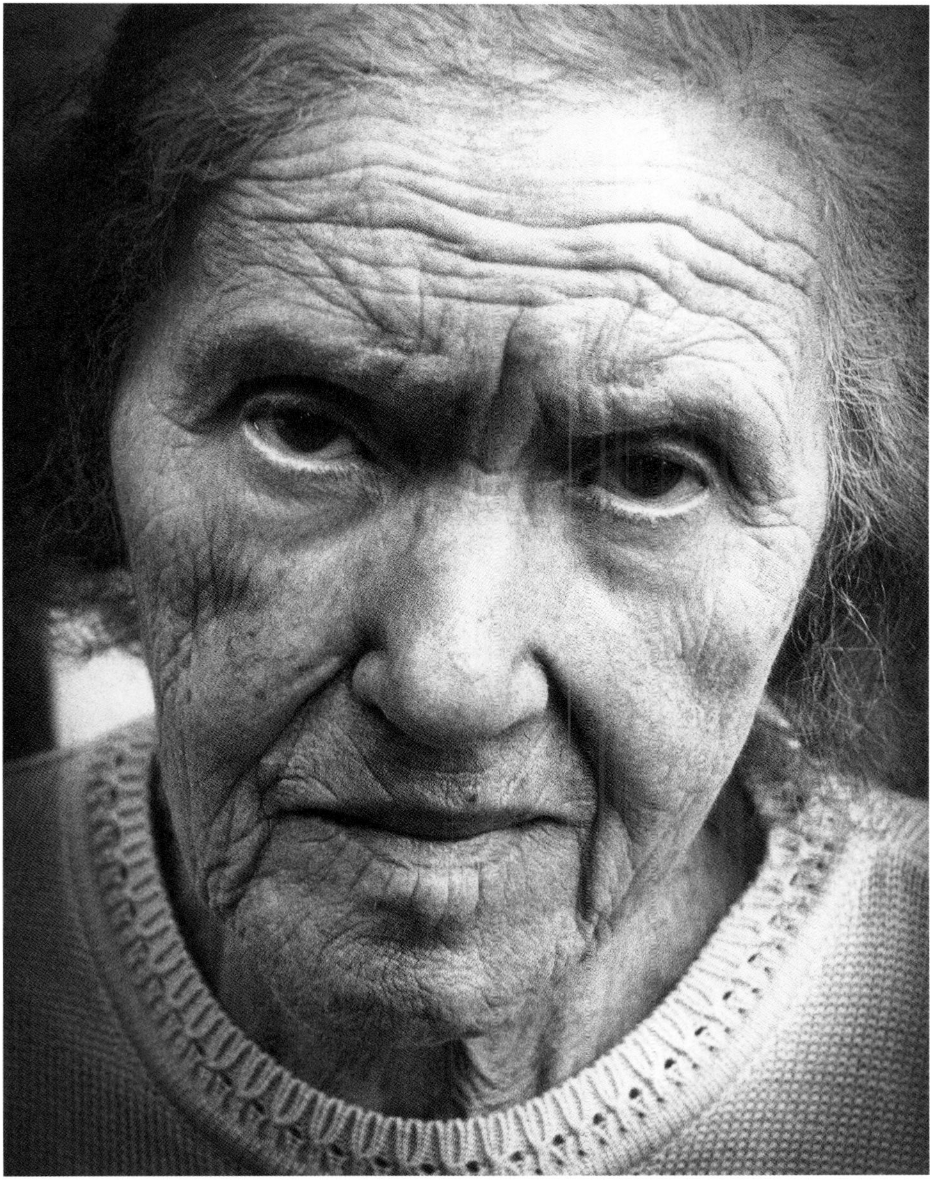

Genė Machatienė. Born 1915

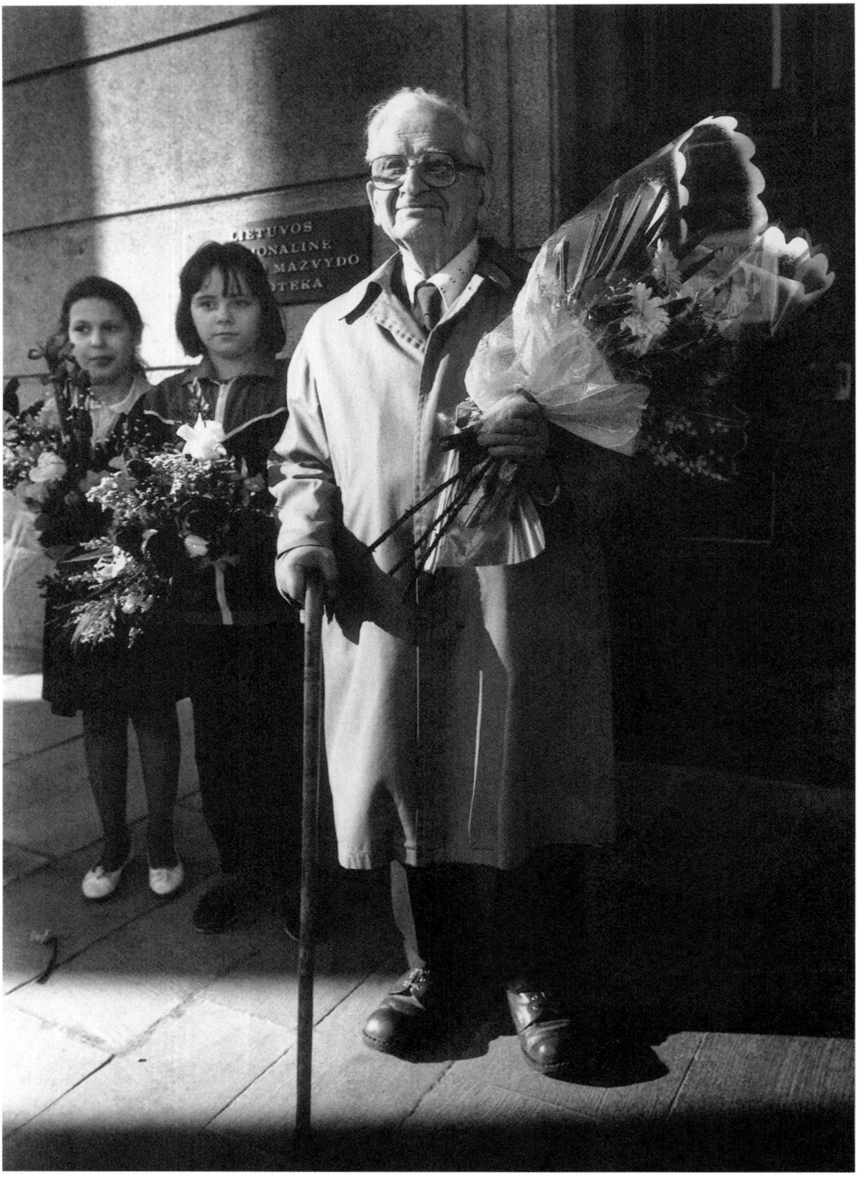

Chackelis Lemchenas. Born 1904

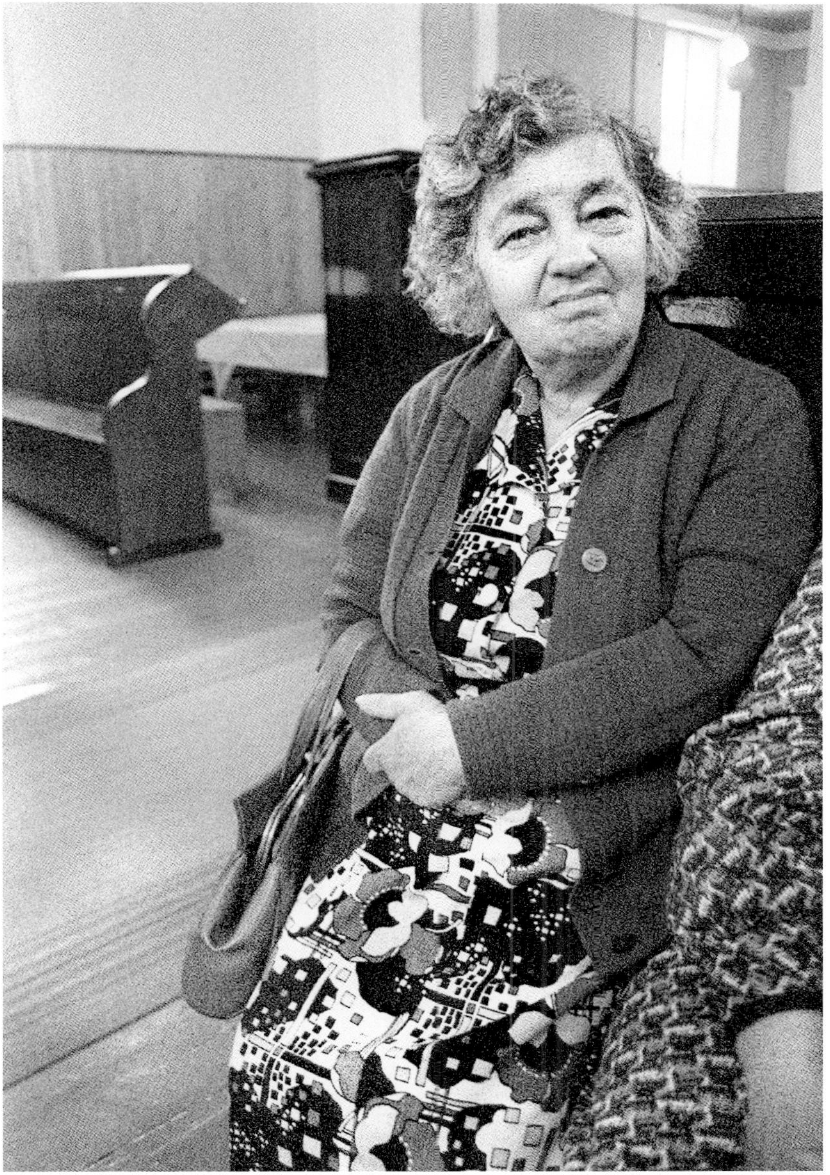

Estera Verbliunskienė. Born 1931

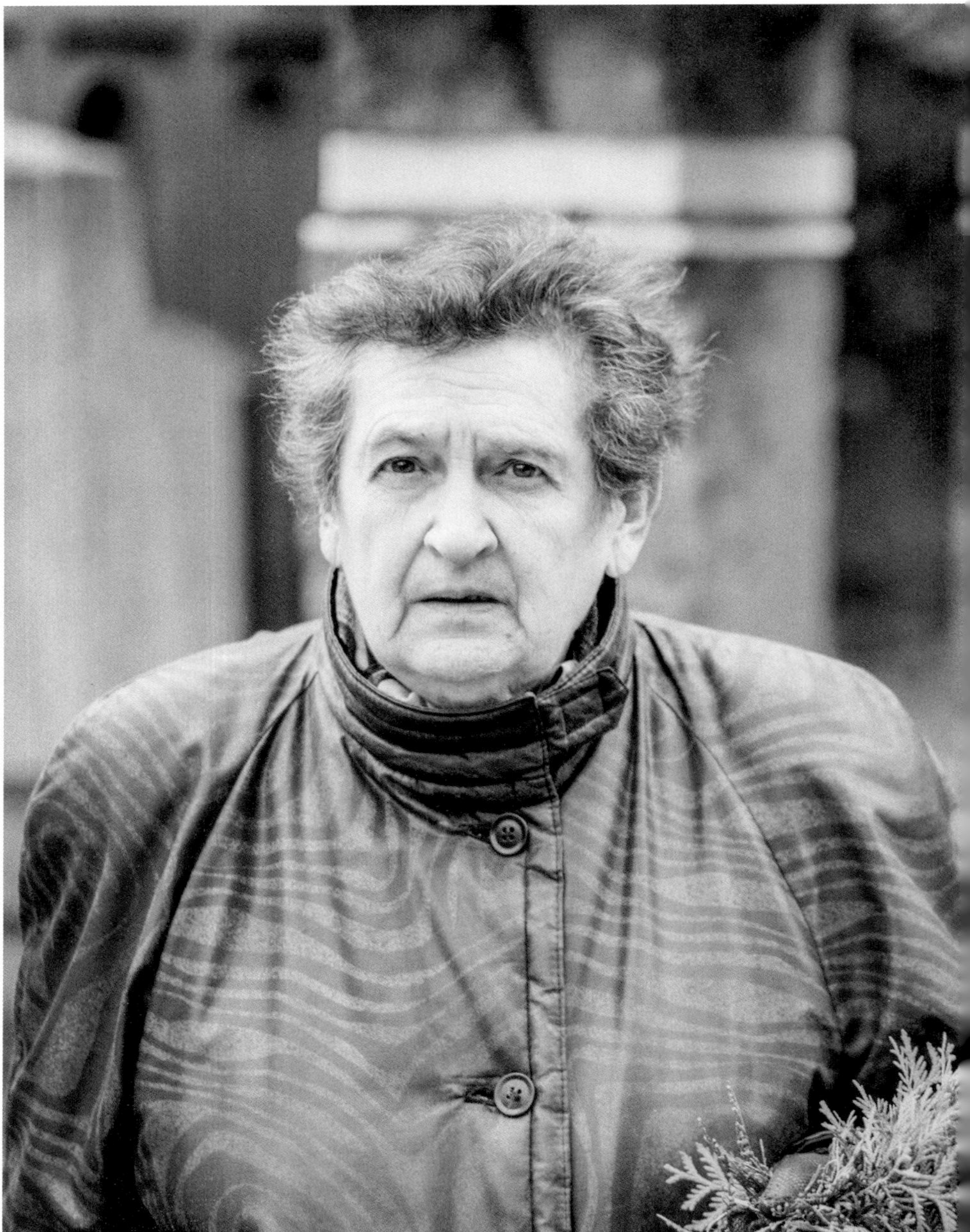

Gita Geršonienė. Born 1925

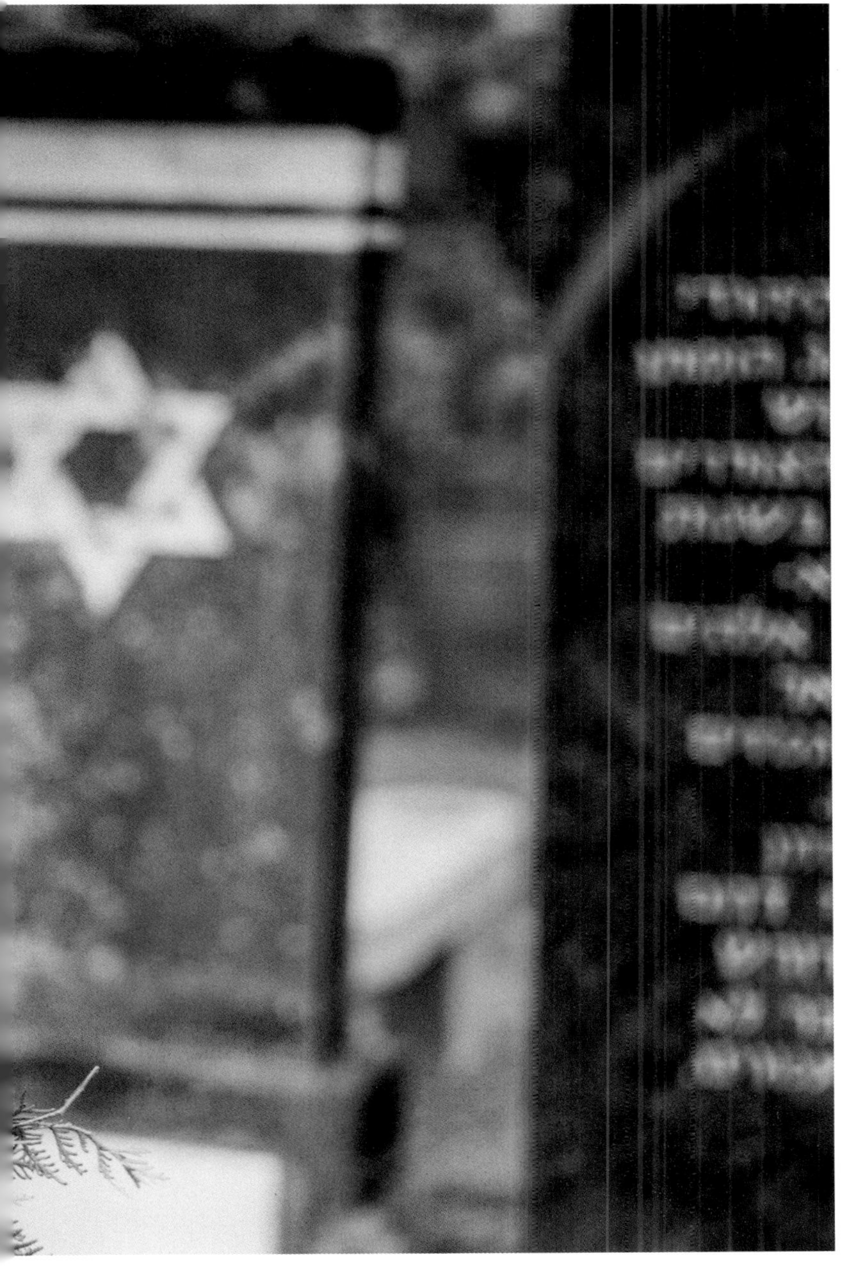

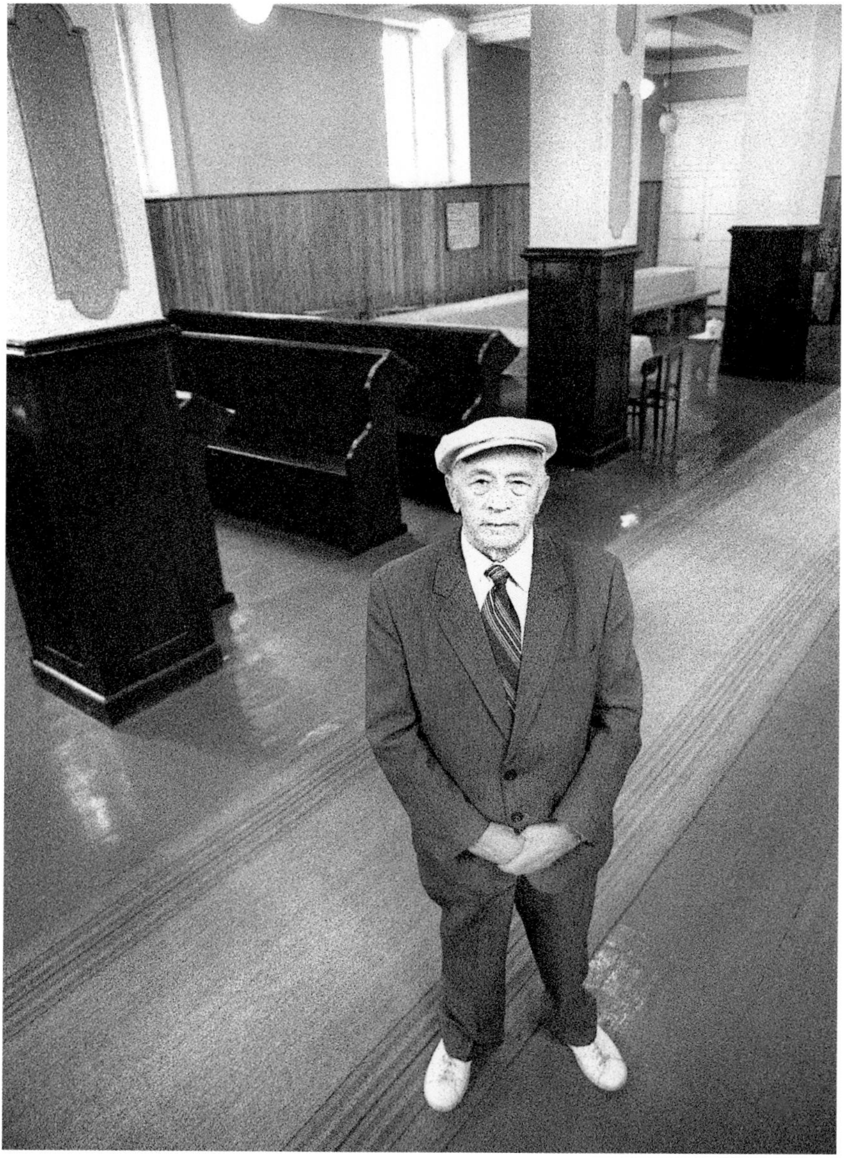

Kasriel Koblenc. Born 1922

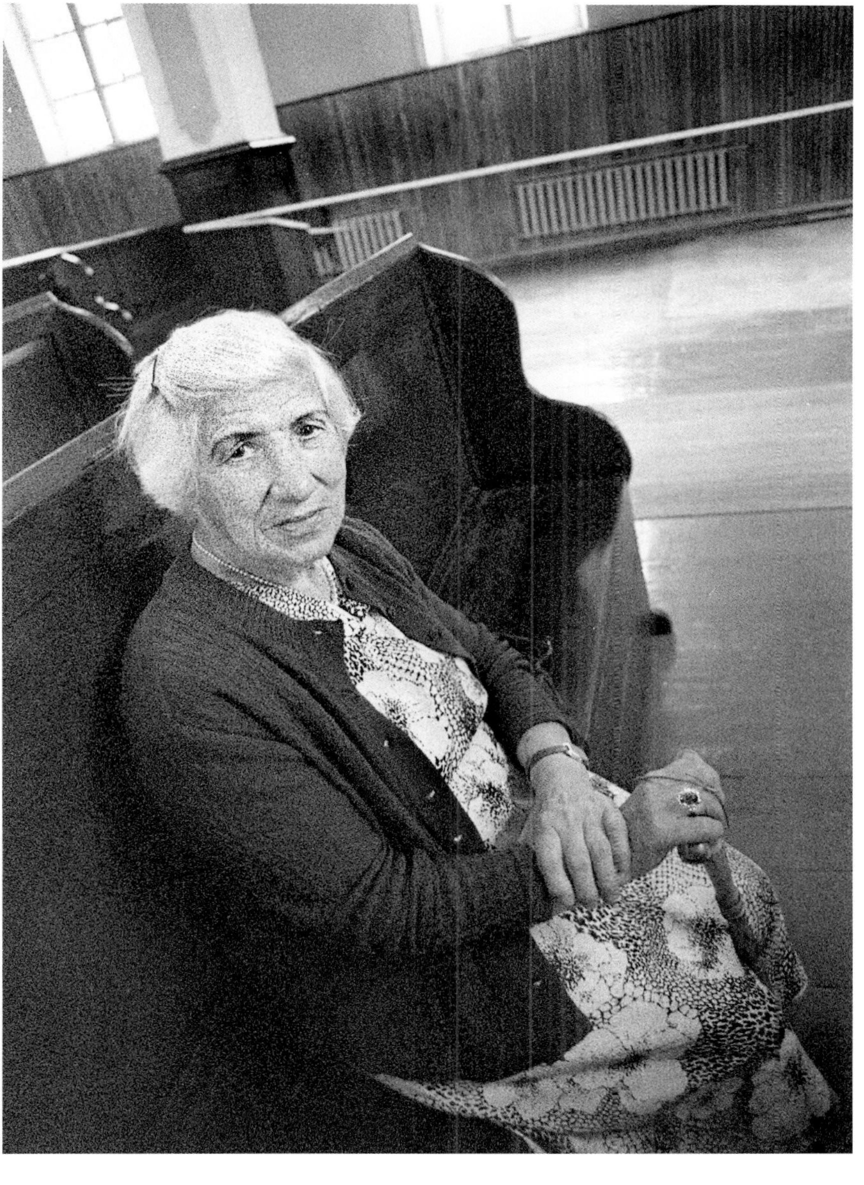

Raisa Kleinaitė. Born 1919

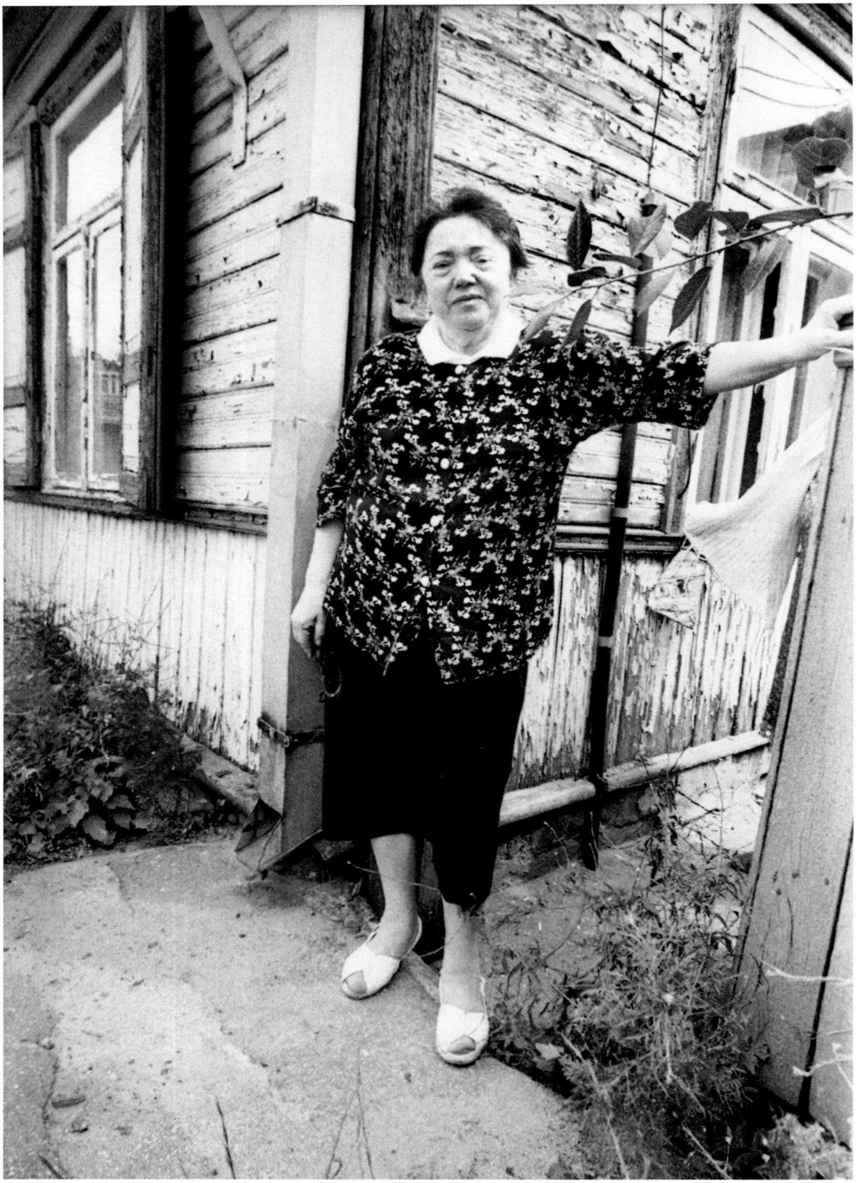

Merė Gotlerytė. Born 1932

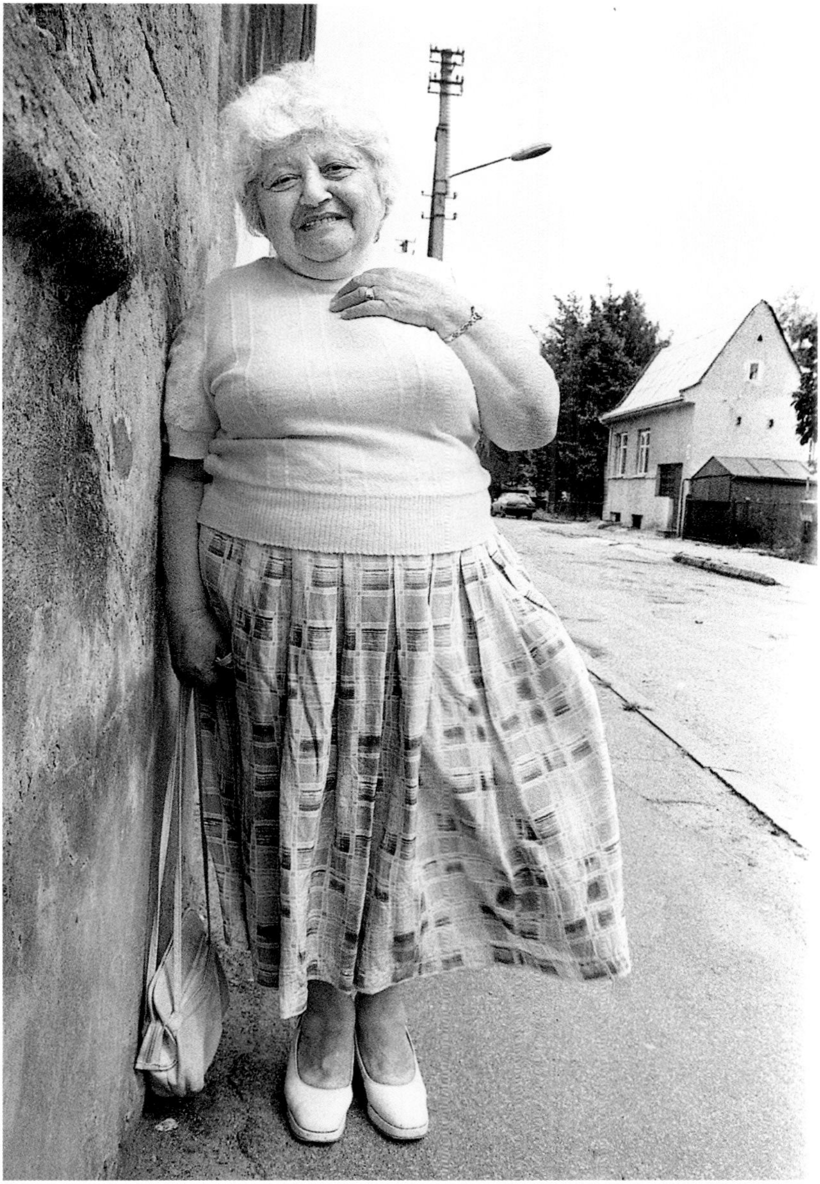

Gita Bargmanienė. Born 1923

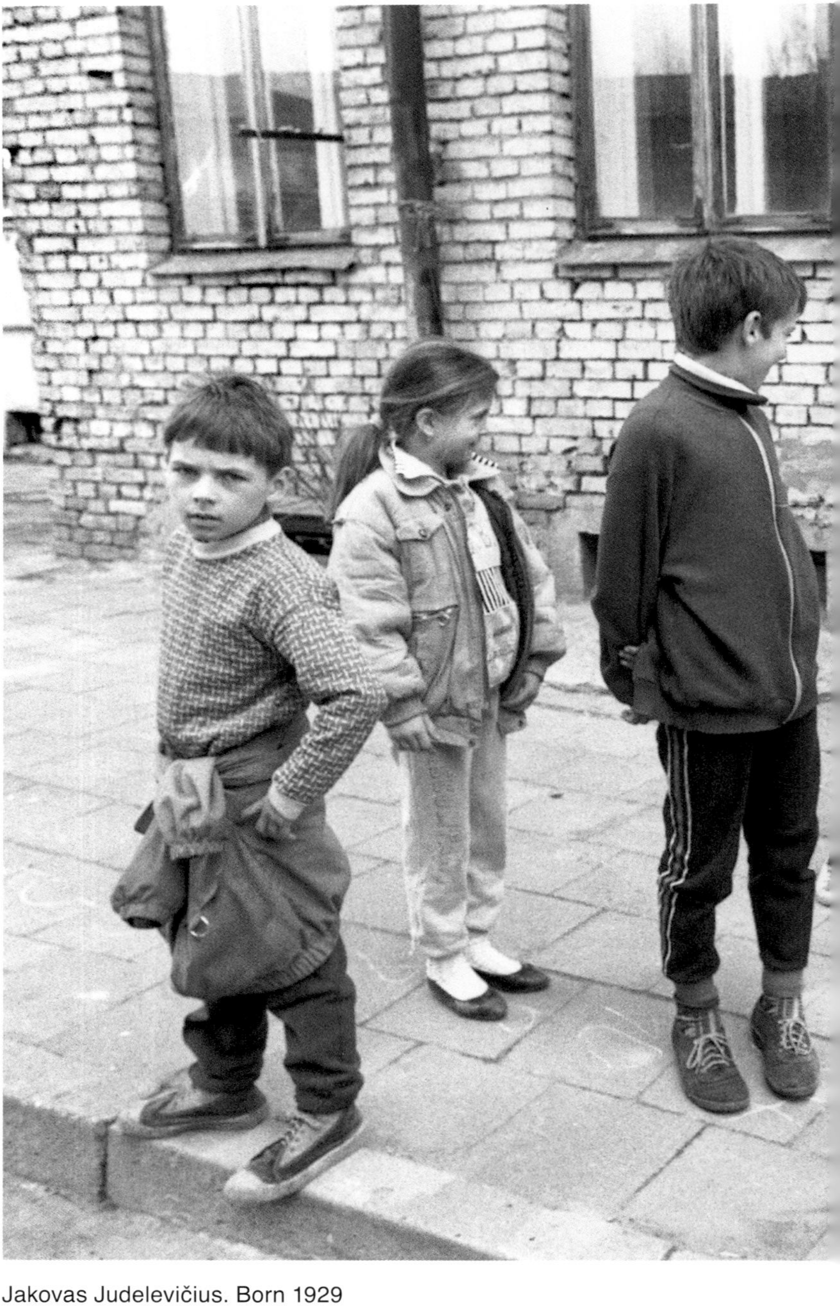

Jakovas Judelevičius. Born 1929

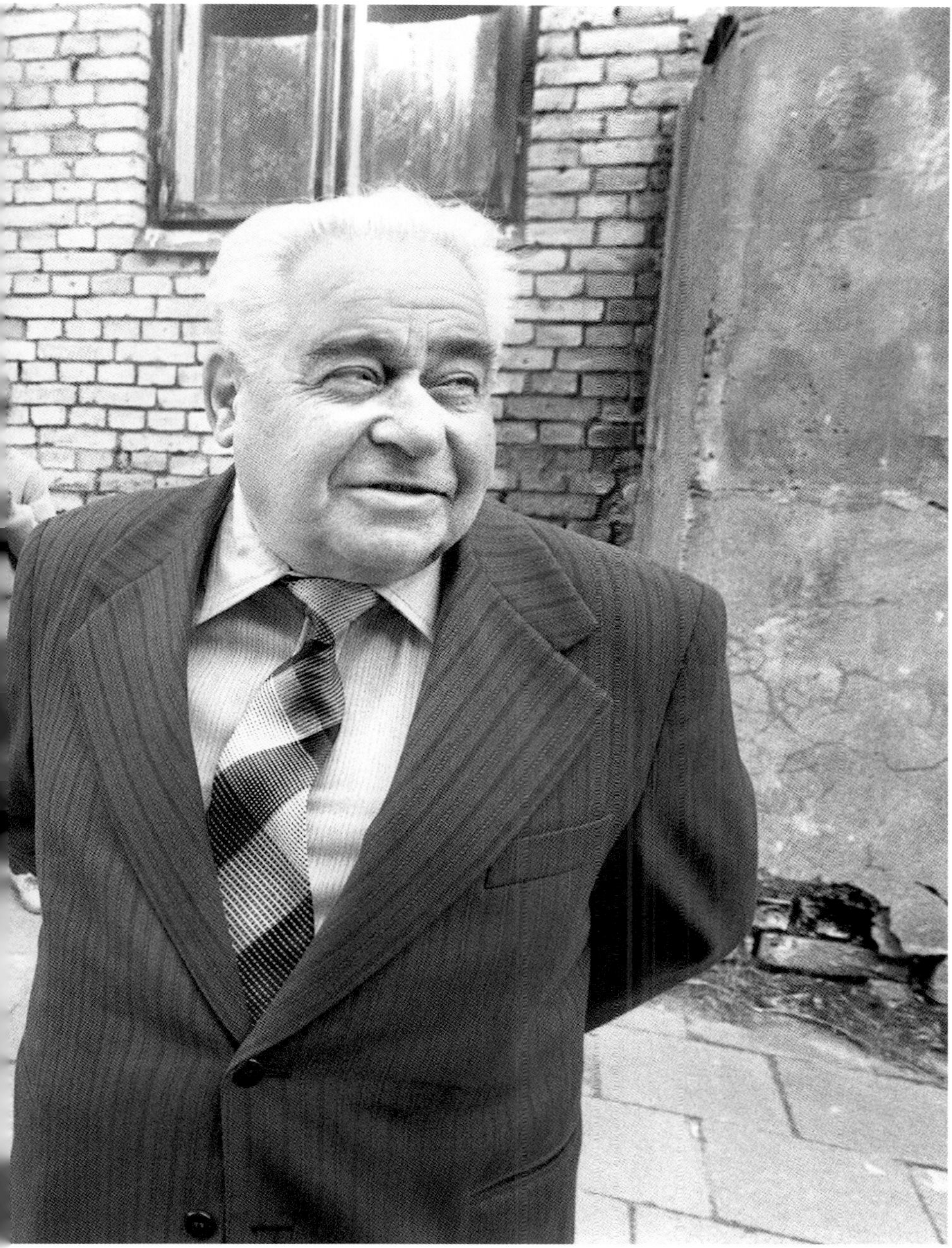

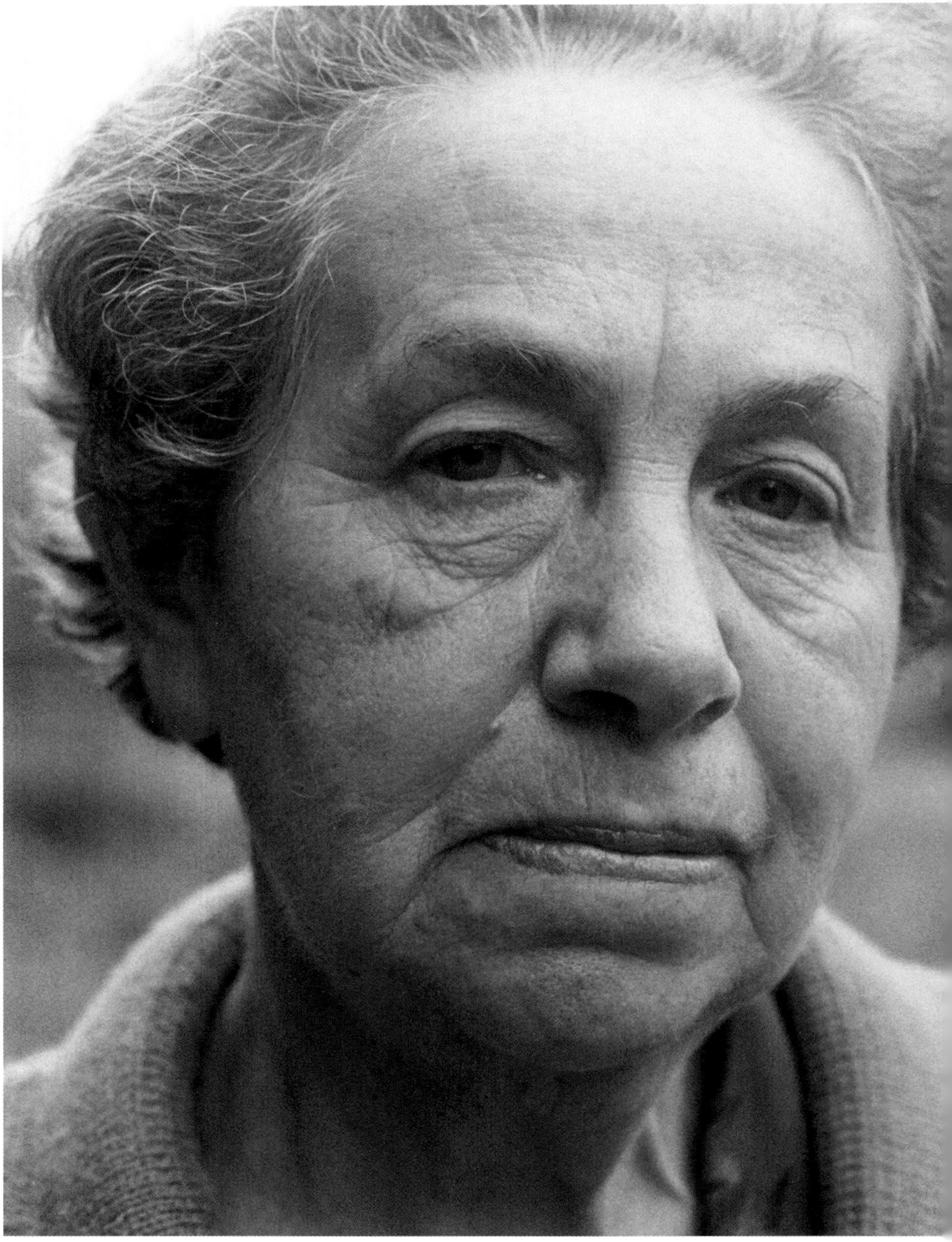

Rachil Šliosberg. Born 1927

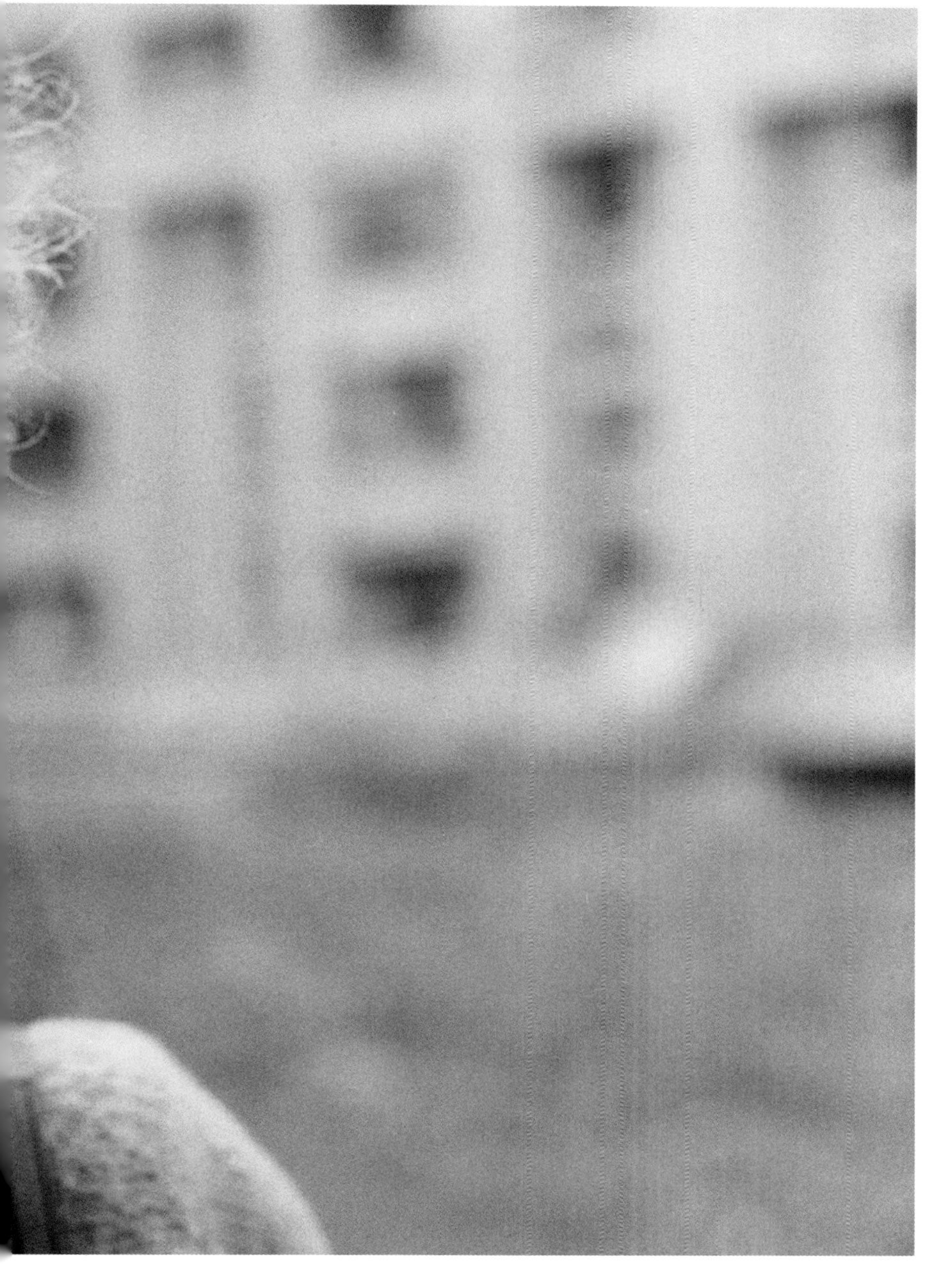

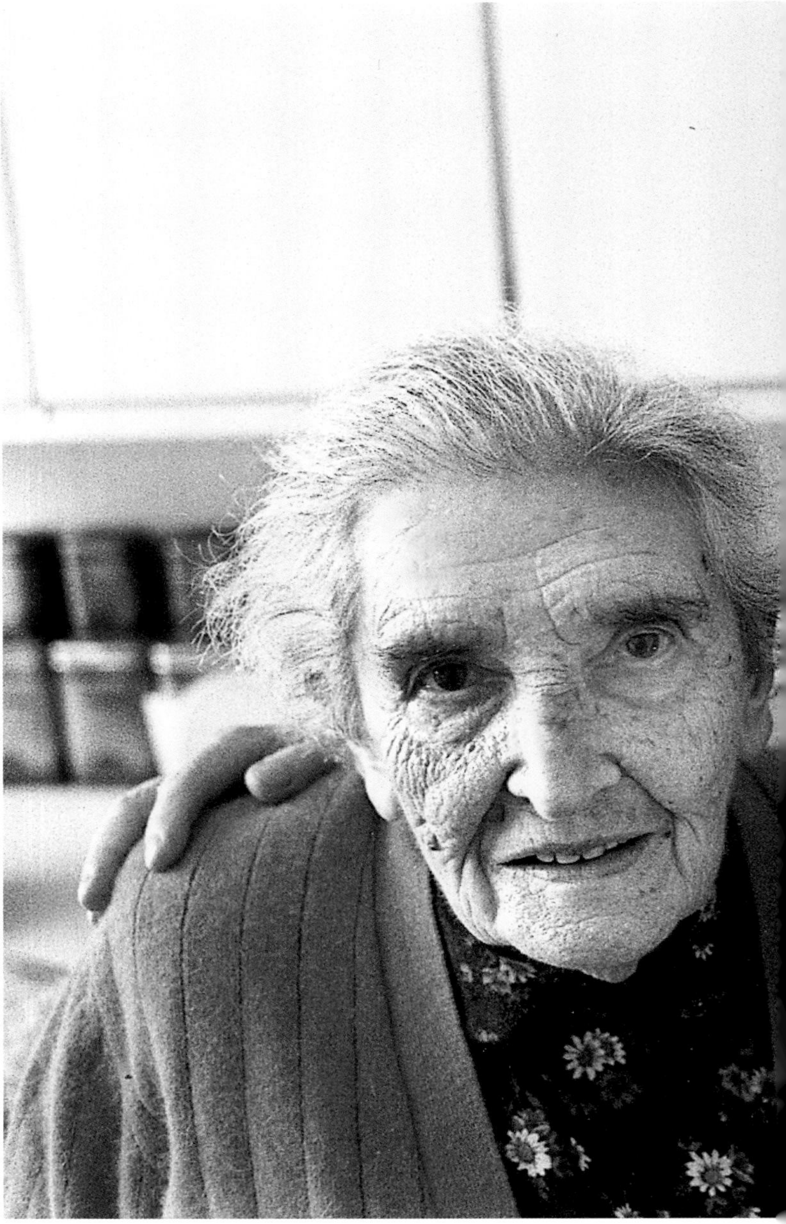

Zinaida Indurskaja. Born 1906

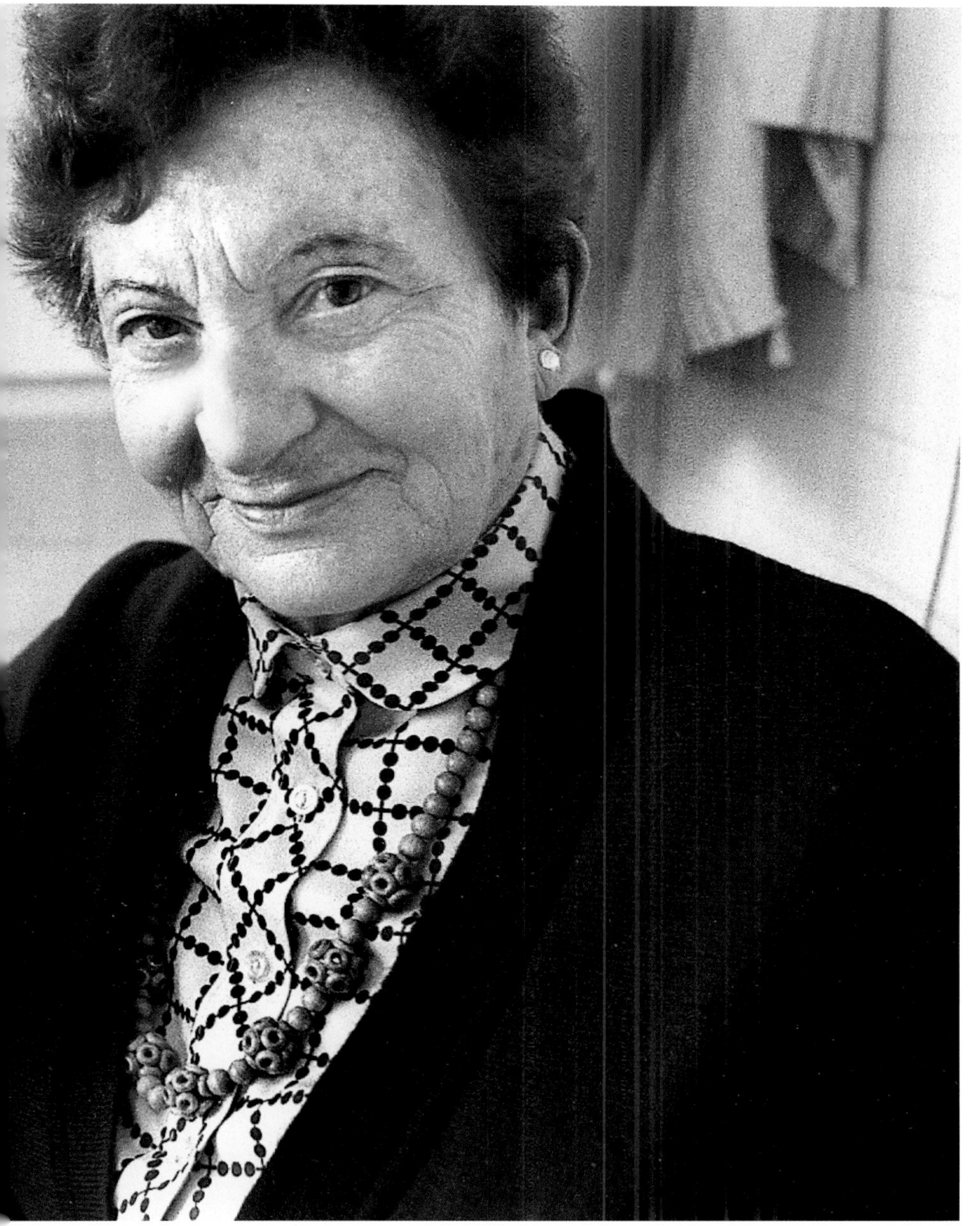

Jėja Finkelšteinaitė. Born 1919

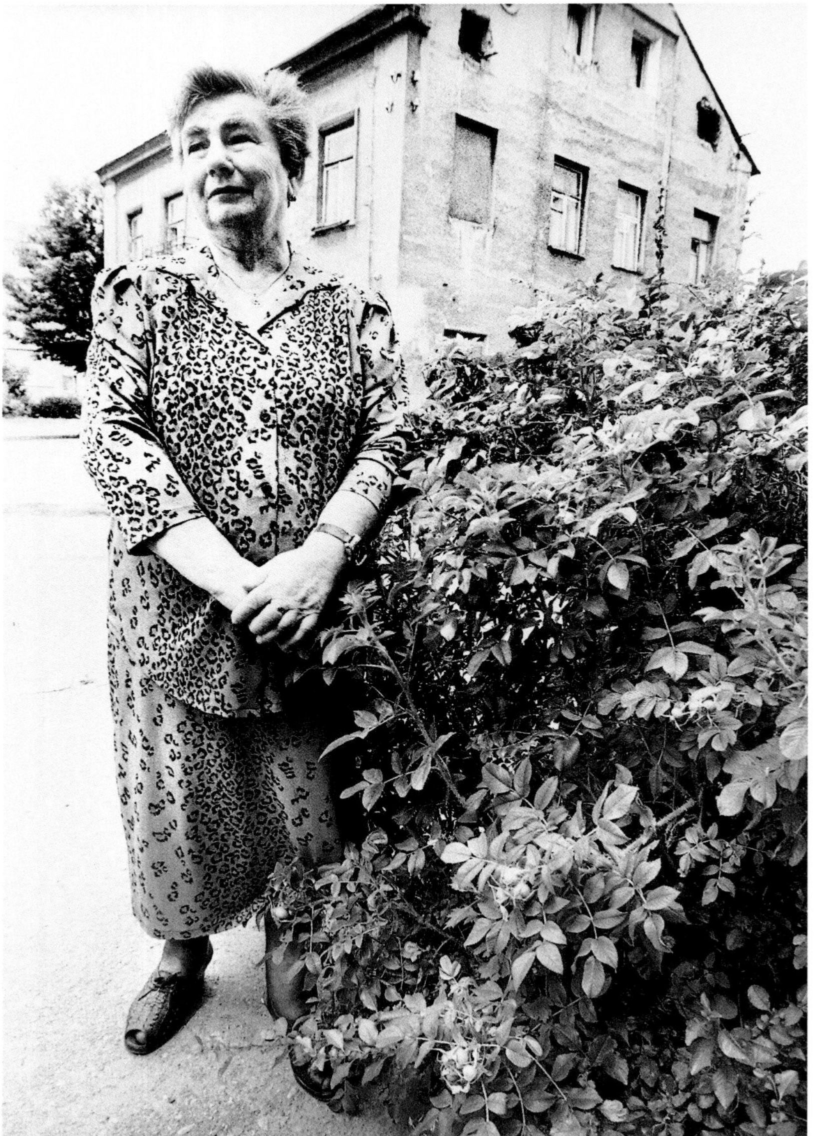

Dobė Rozenbergienė. Born 1928

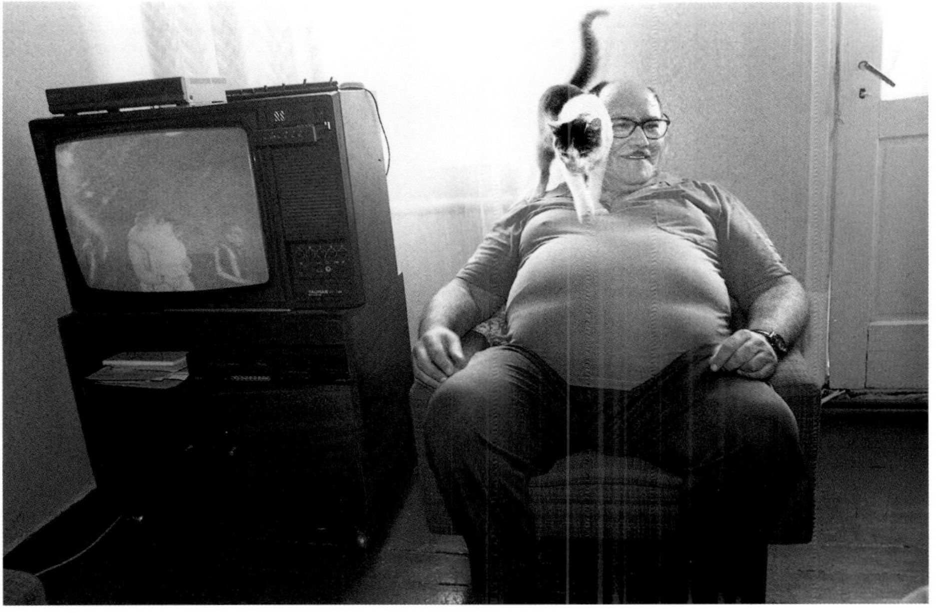

Jakovas Lopianskis. Born 1940

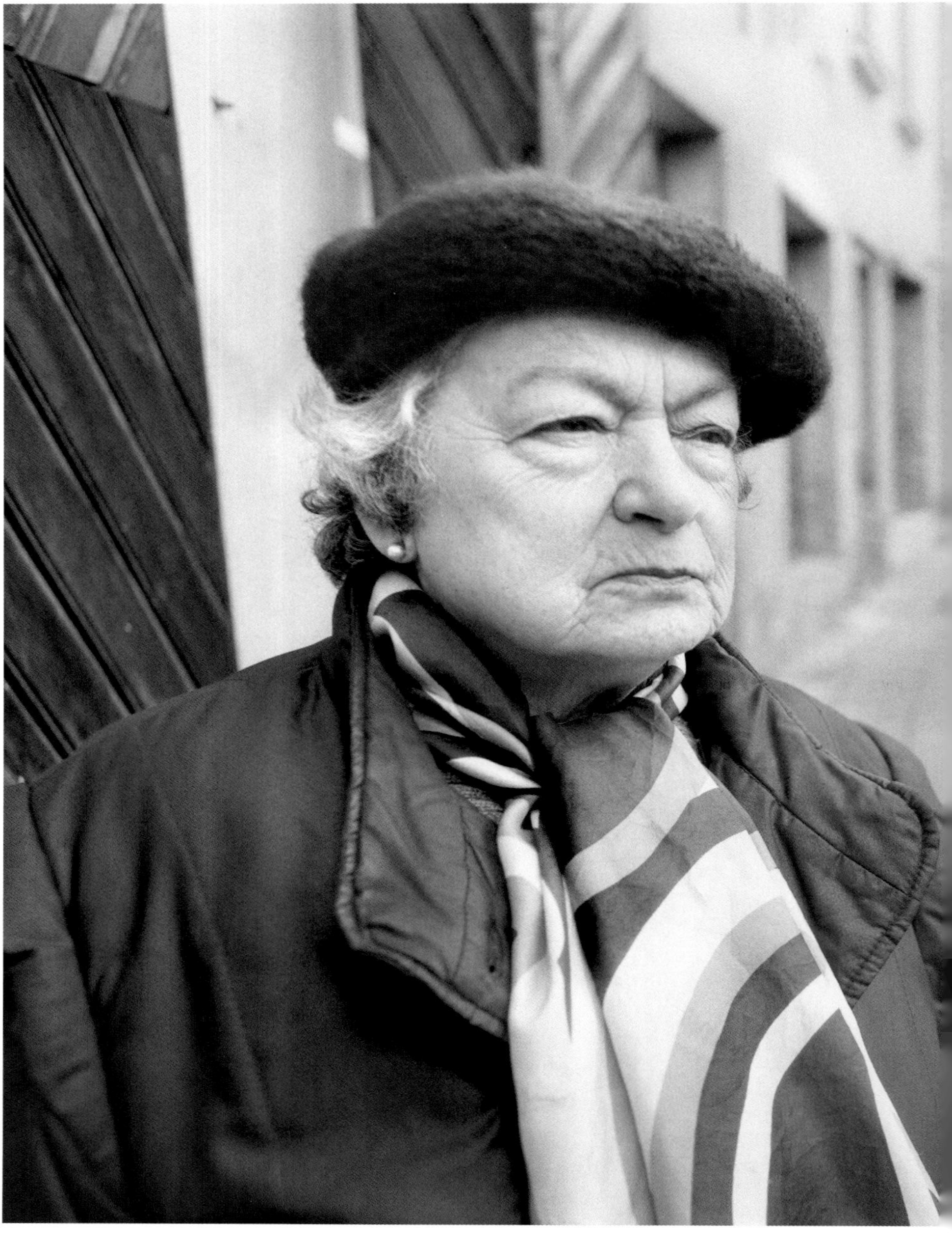

Emiloija Ožinskienė. Born 1924

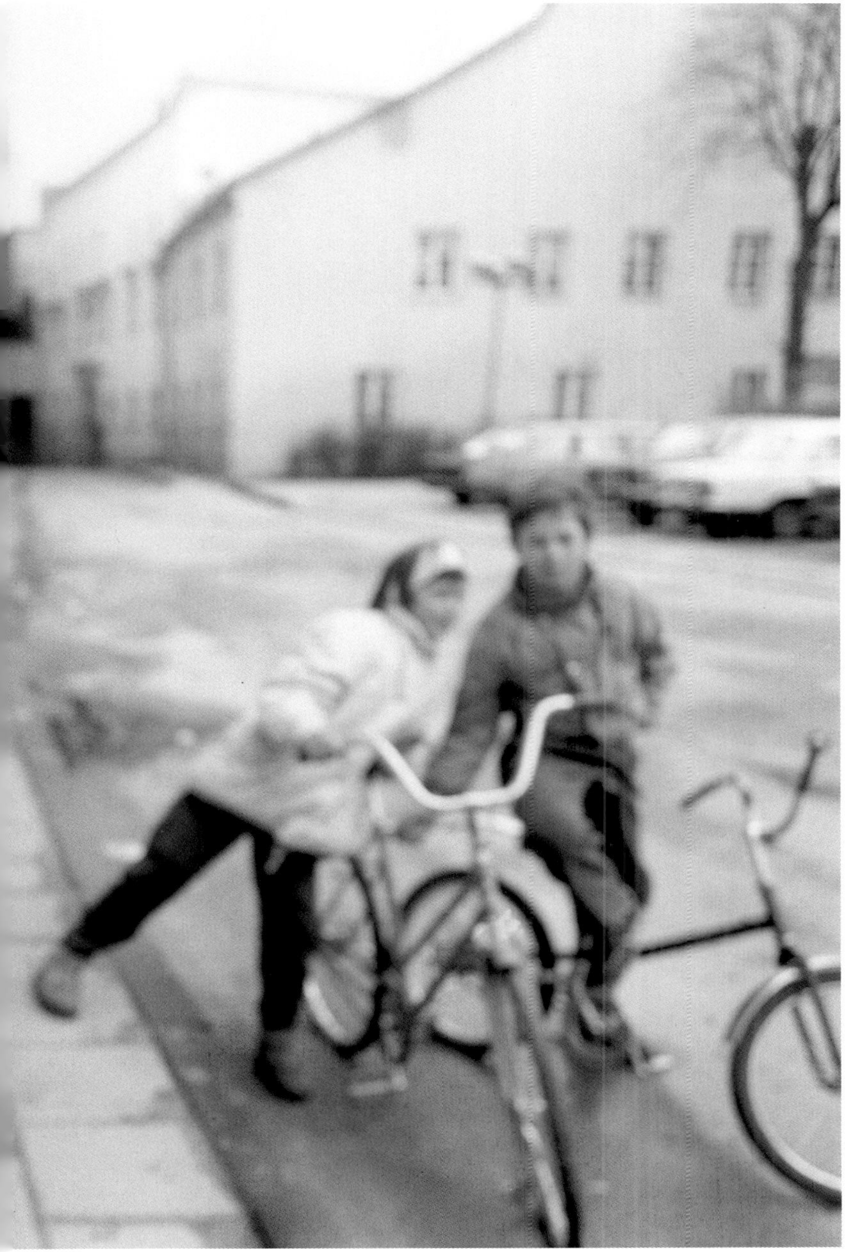

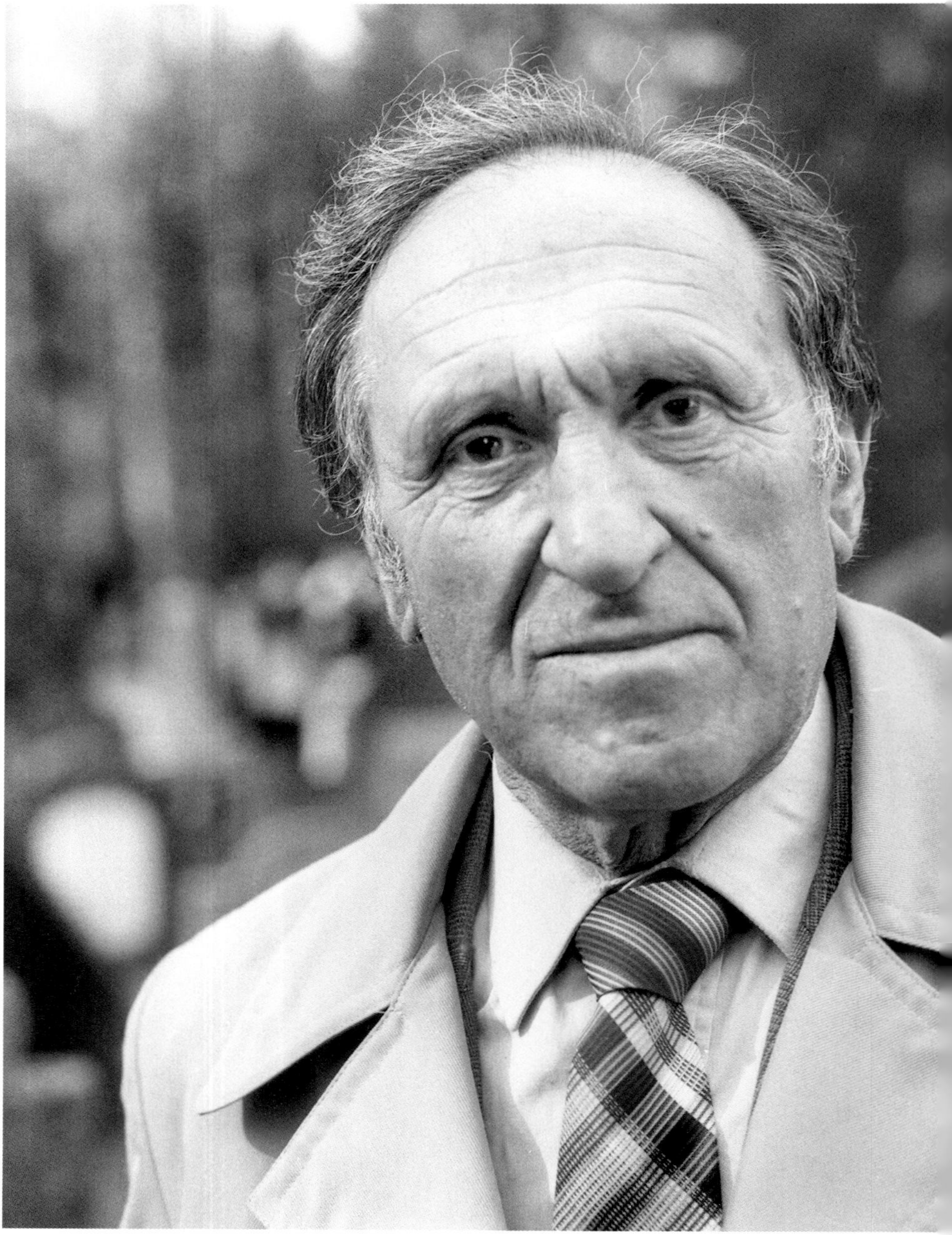

Mejeris Gercmanas. Born 1923

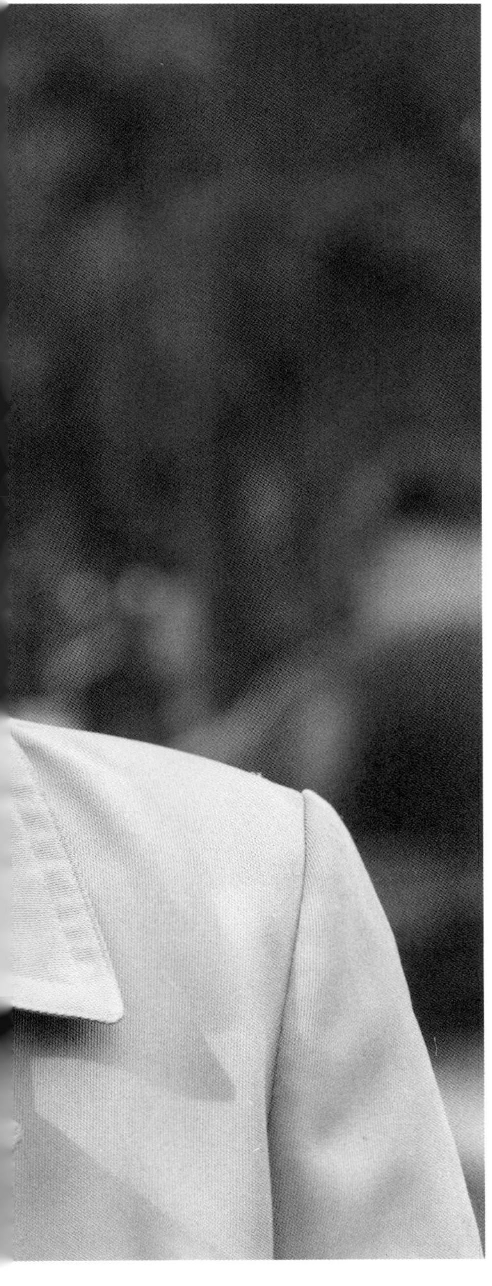

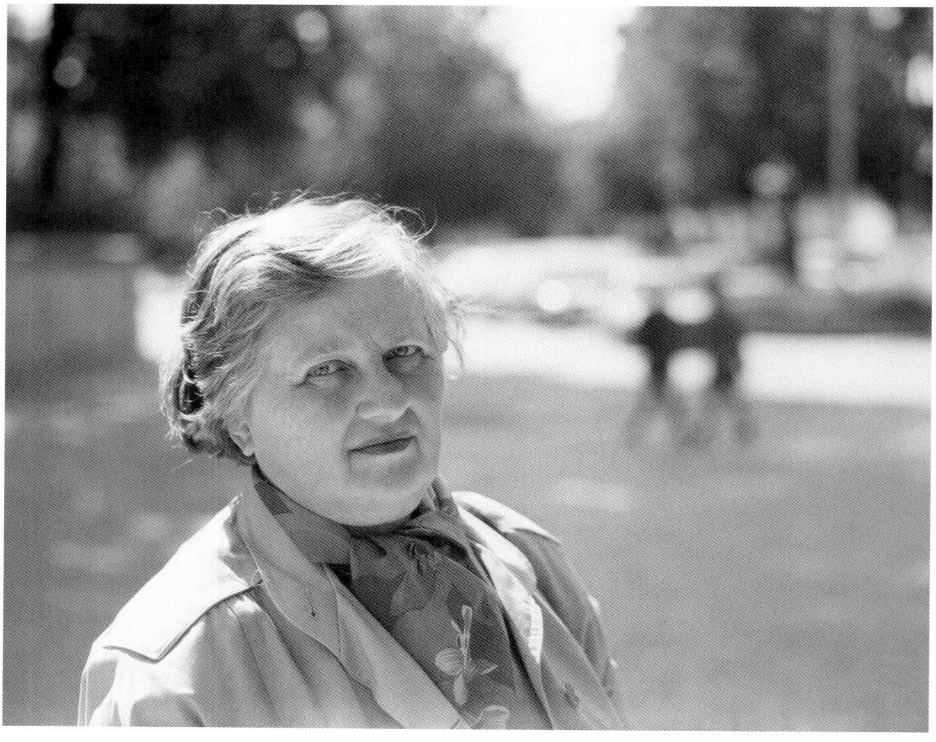

Bliuma Taločkienė. Born 1934

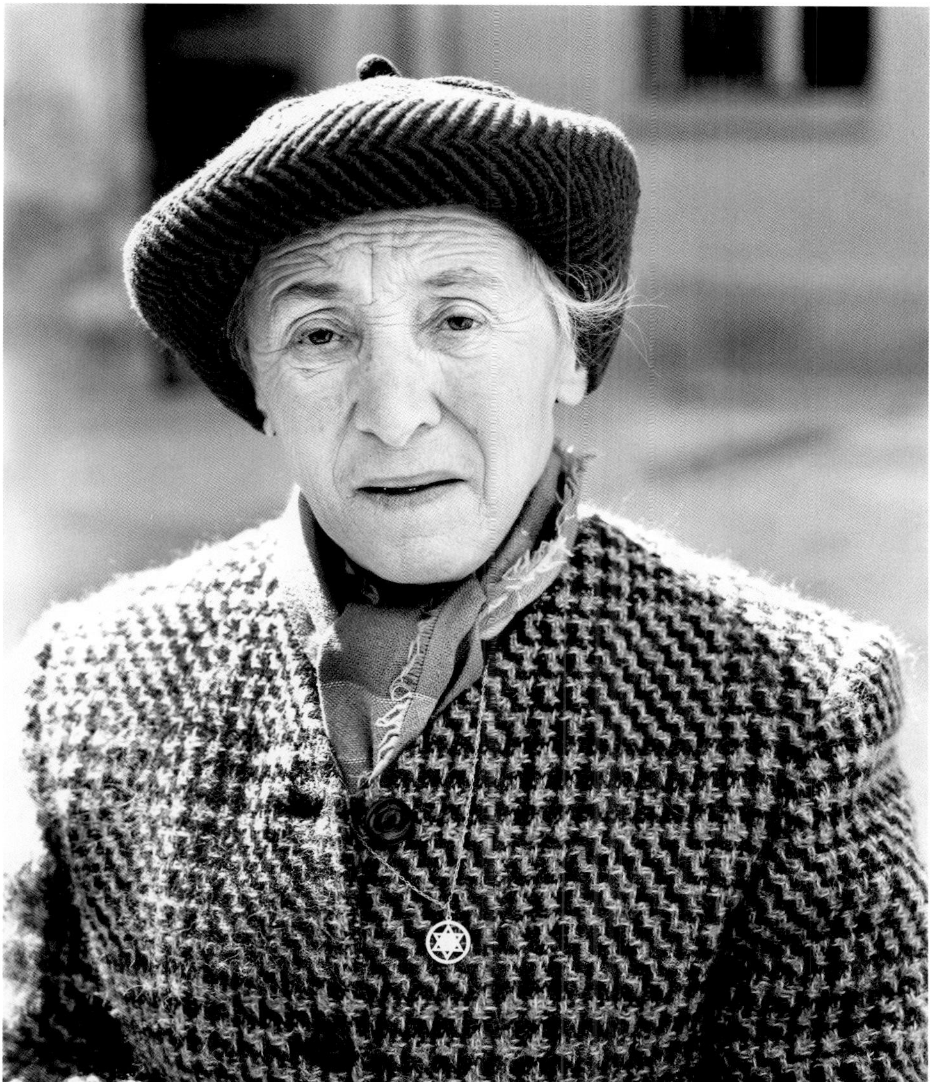

Zelda Gurvič. Born 1919

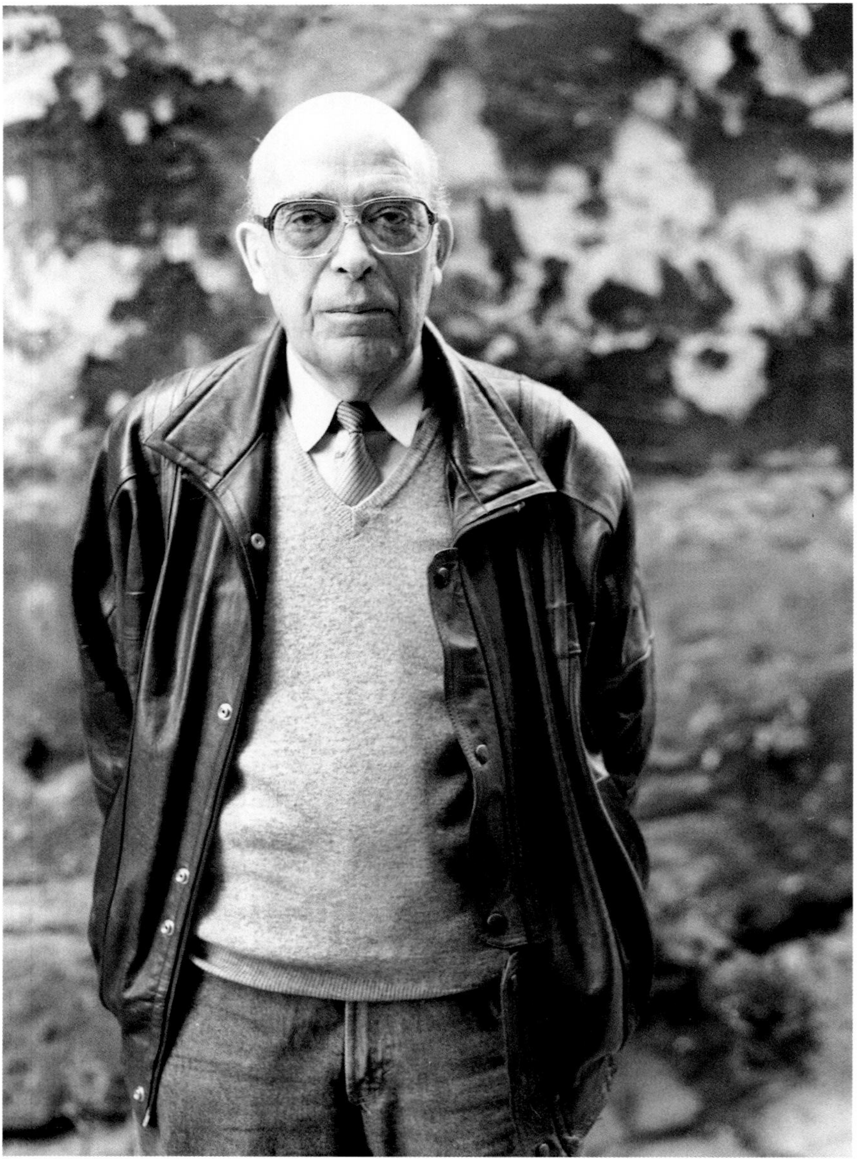

Dovydas Šapiro. Born 1922

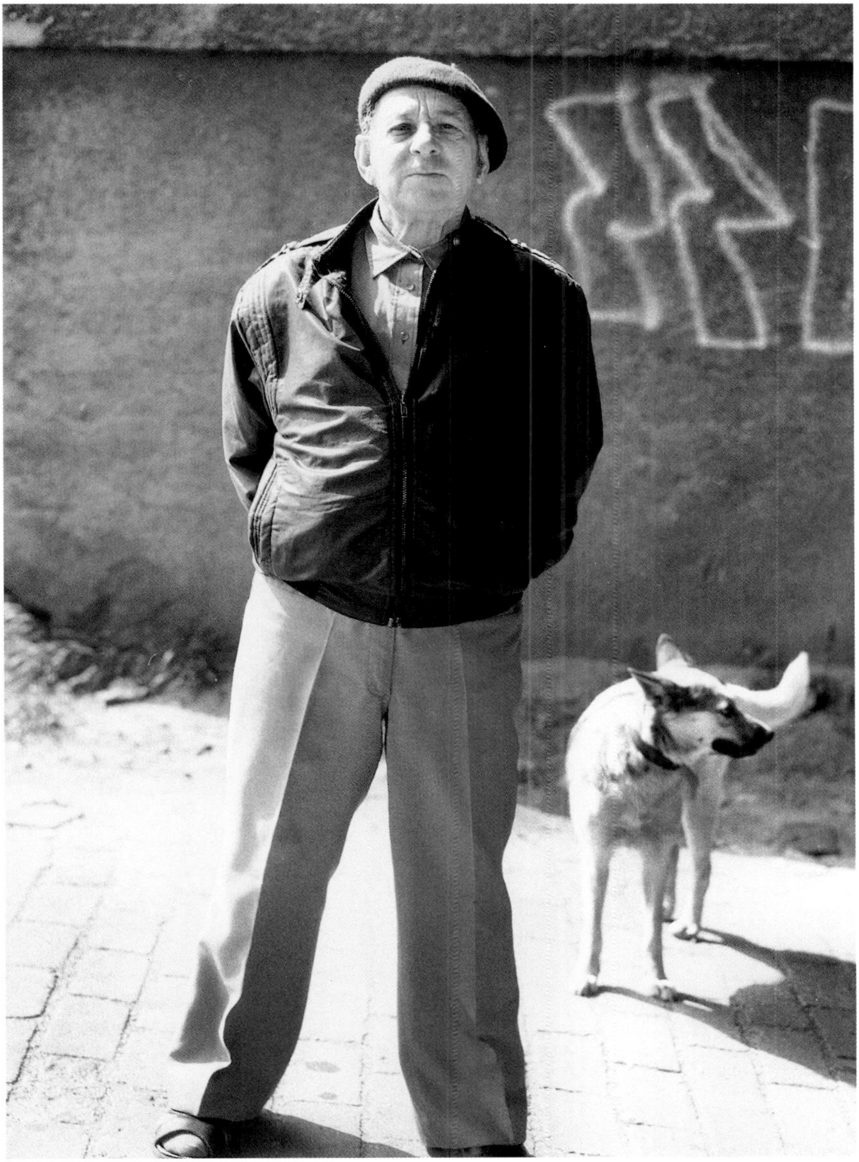

Šapsai Cholen. Born 1925

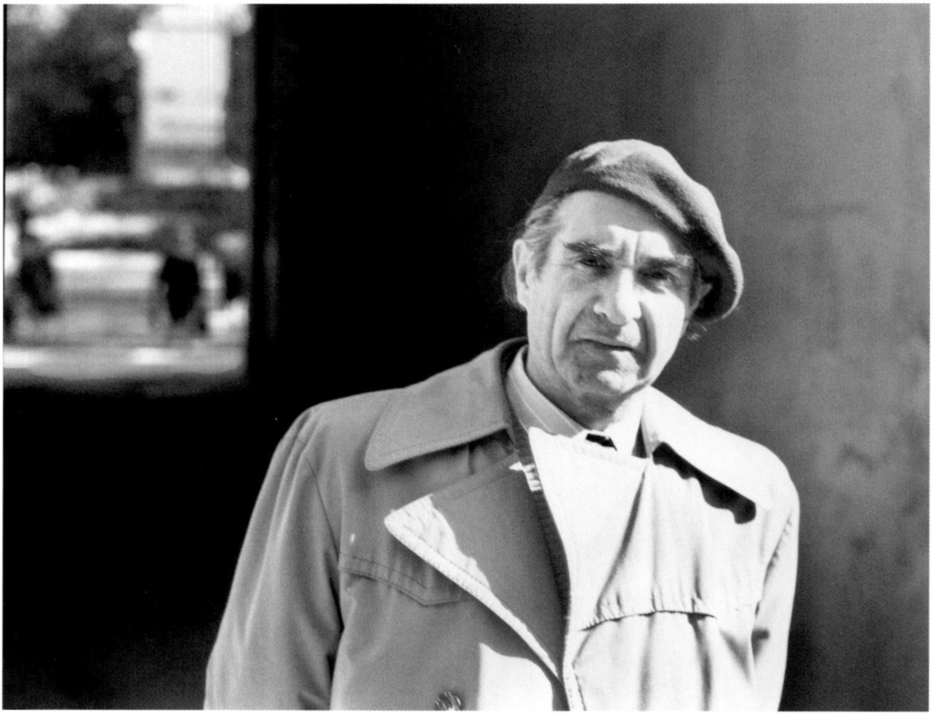

Grigorijus Smoliakovas. Born 1922

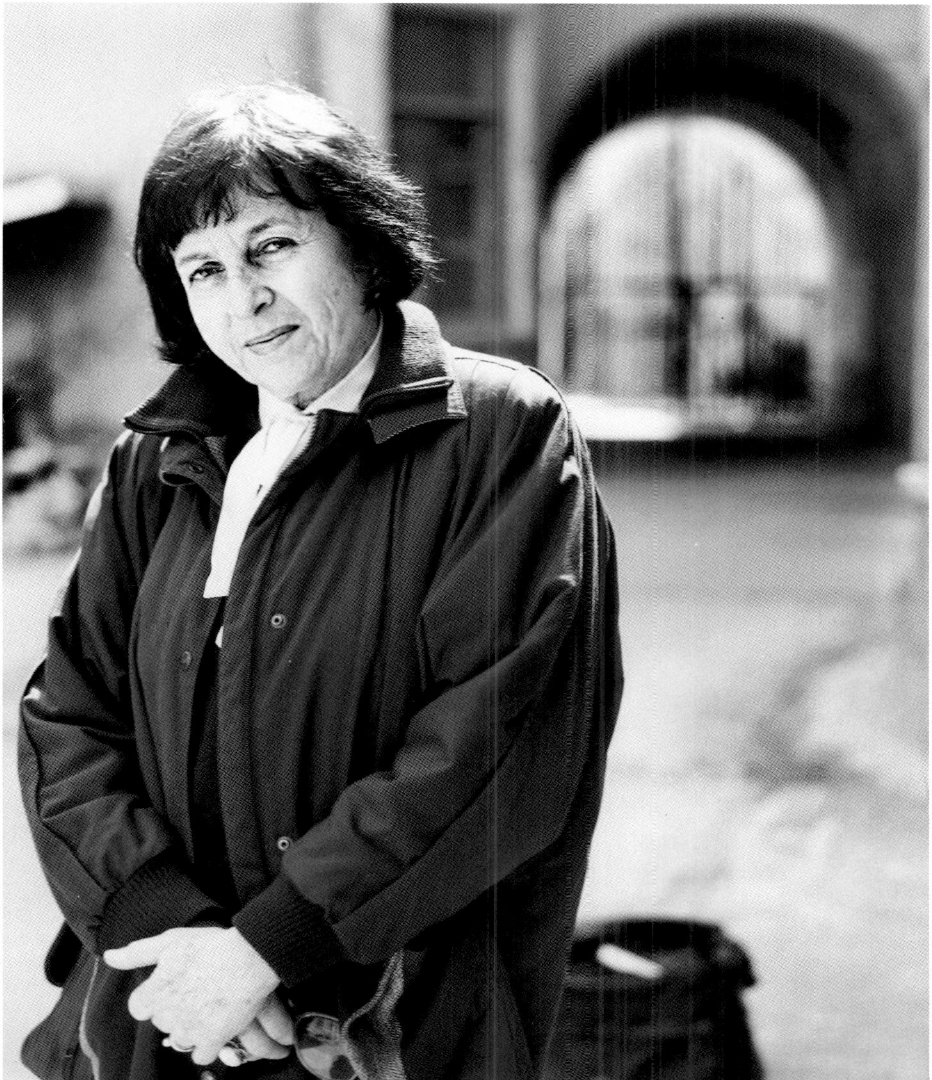

Irena Veisaitė. Born 1928

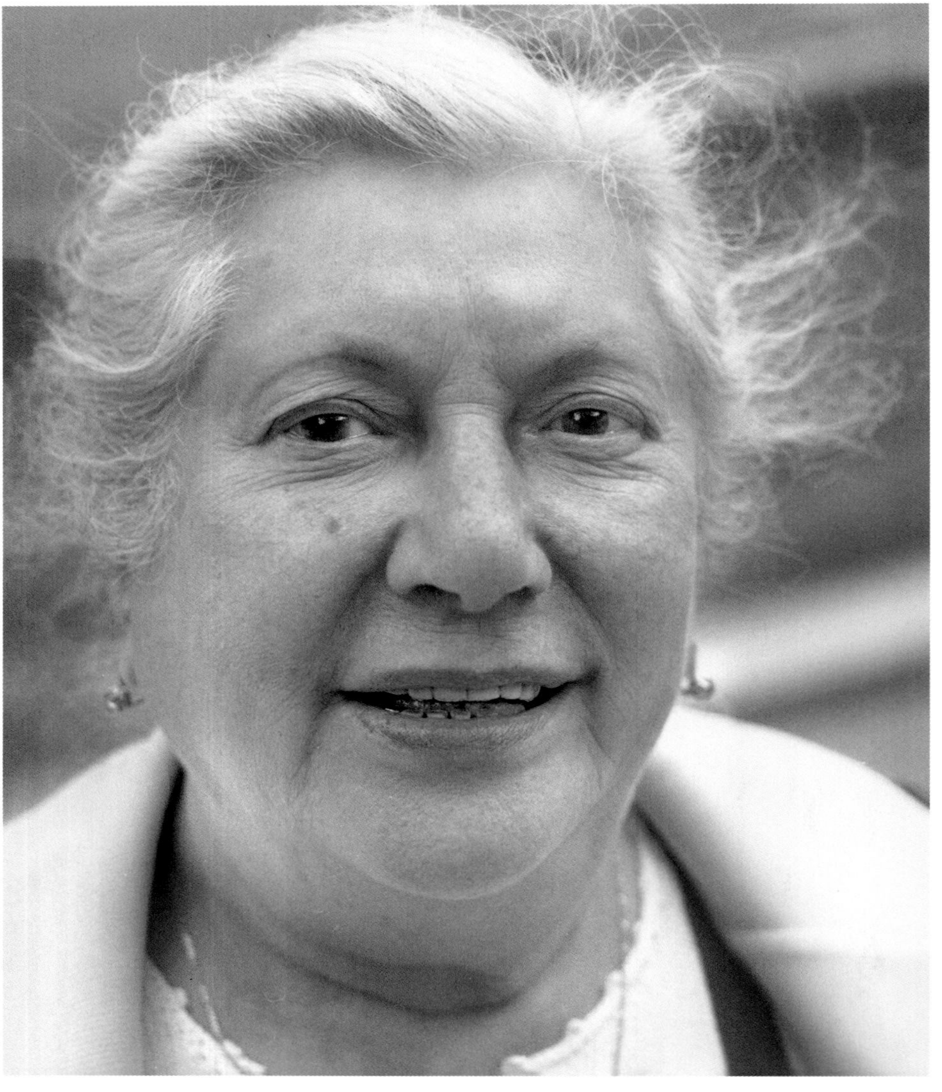

Riša Šmuklerienė. Born 1923

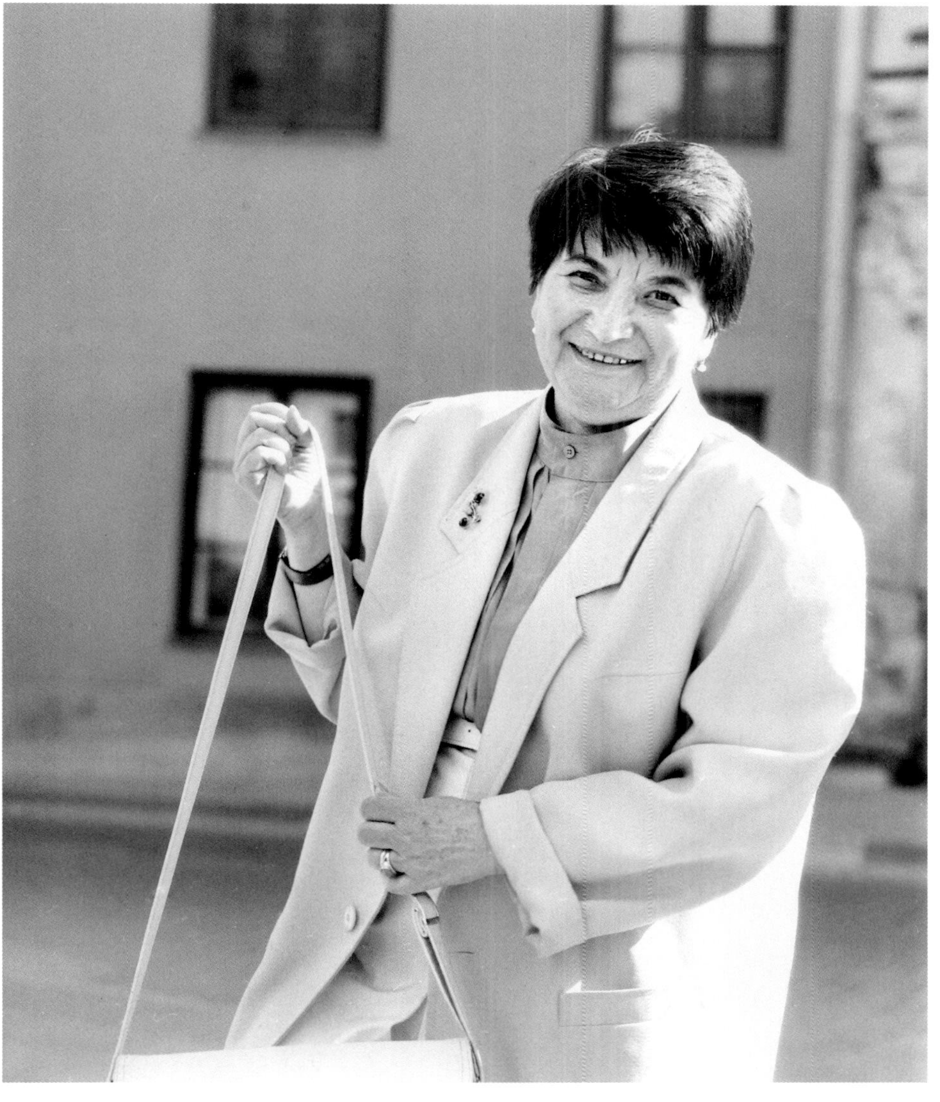

Gita Grinmanienė. Born 1939

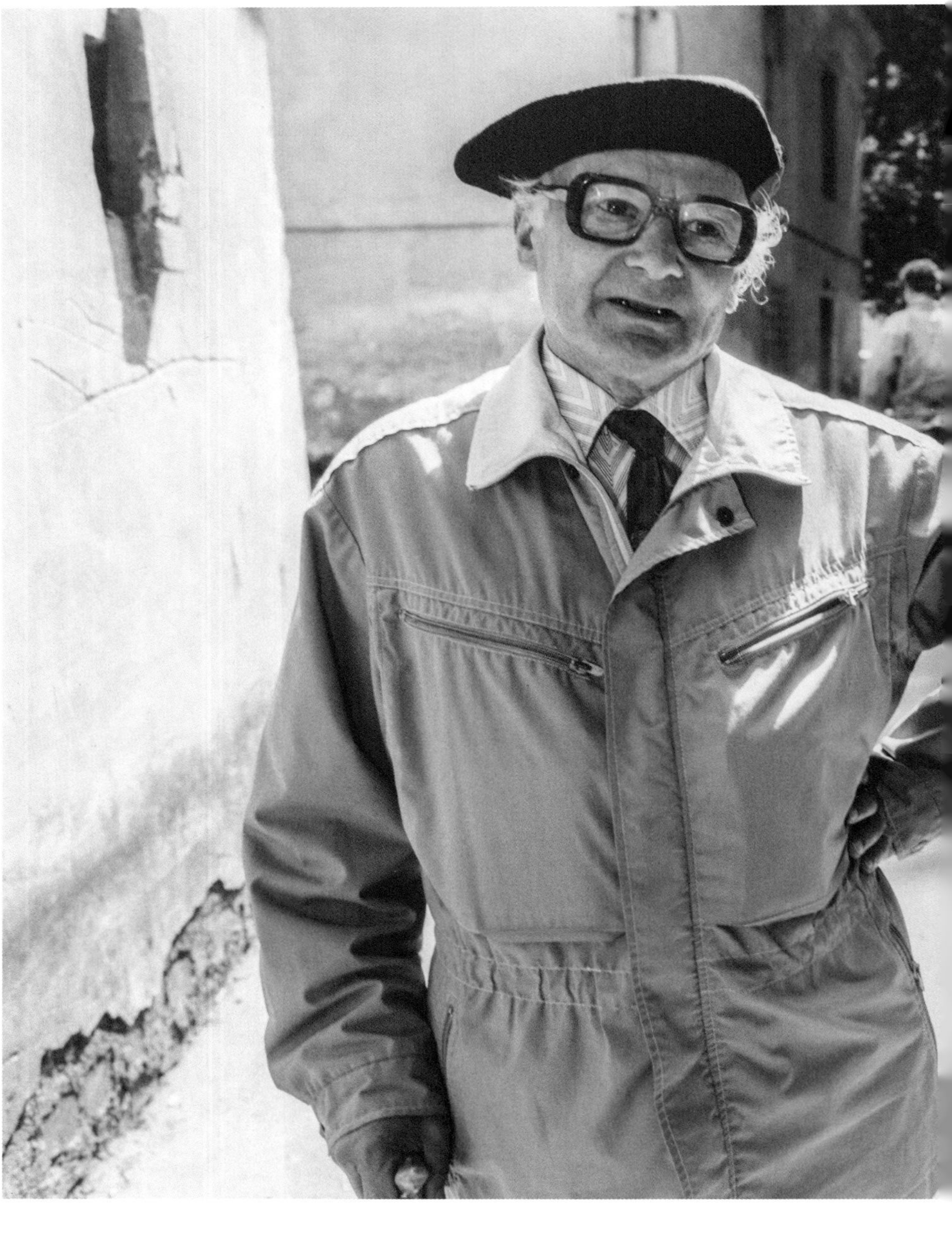

Moisej Gegužinskis. Born 1924

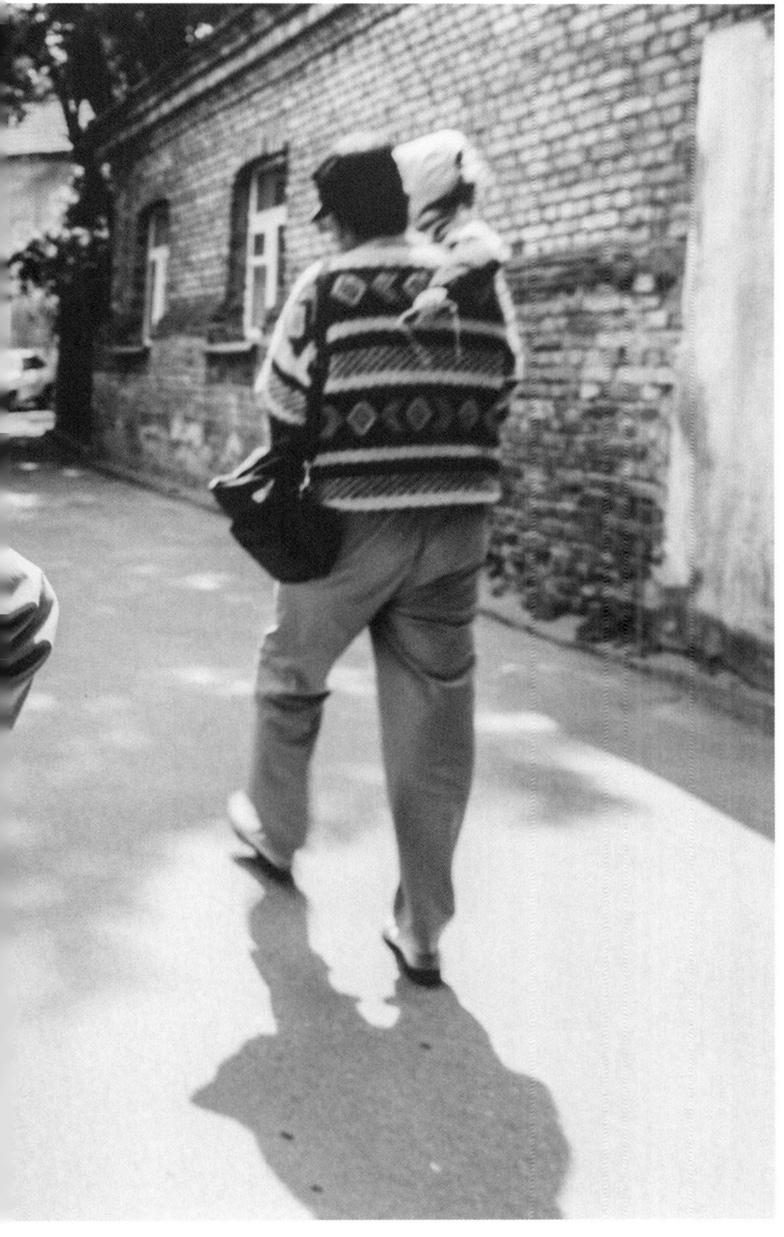

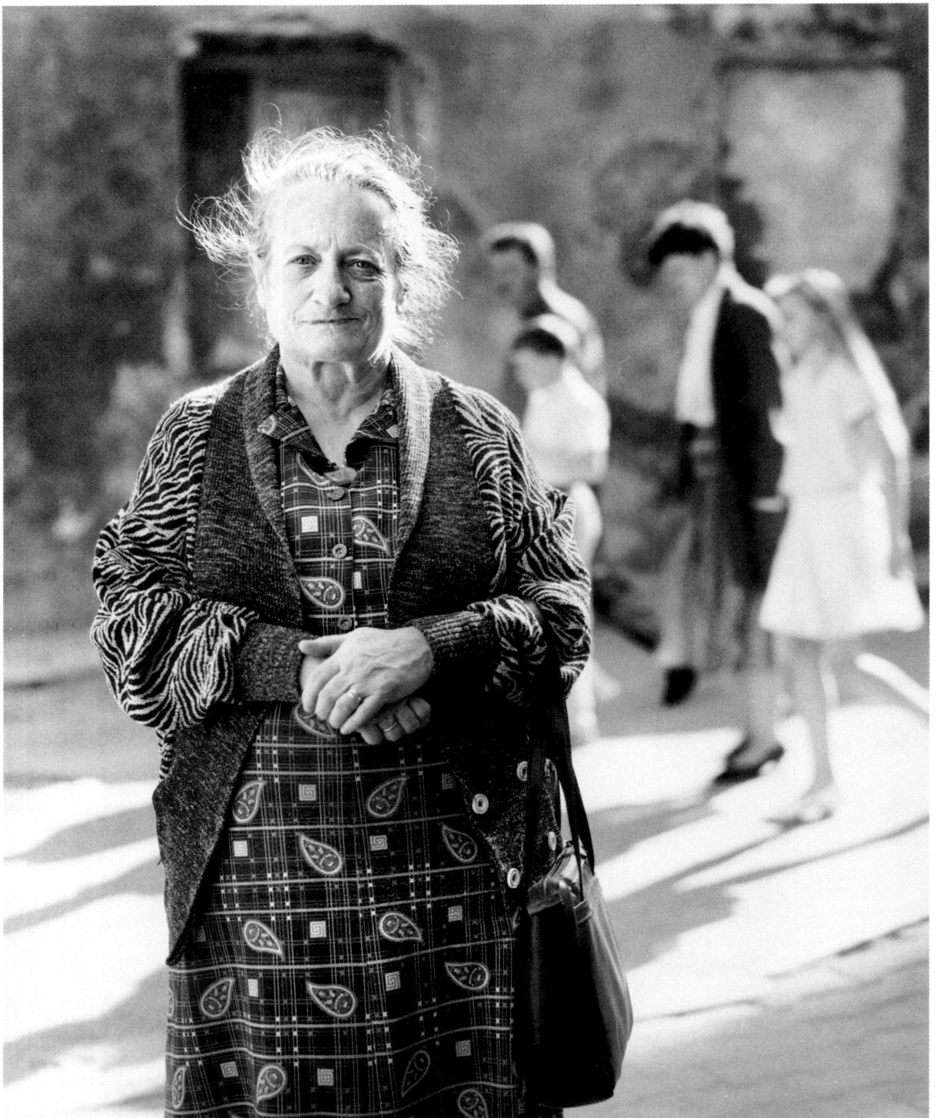

Maja Vysockaja. Born 1936

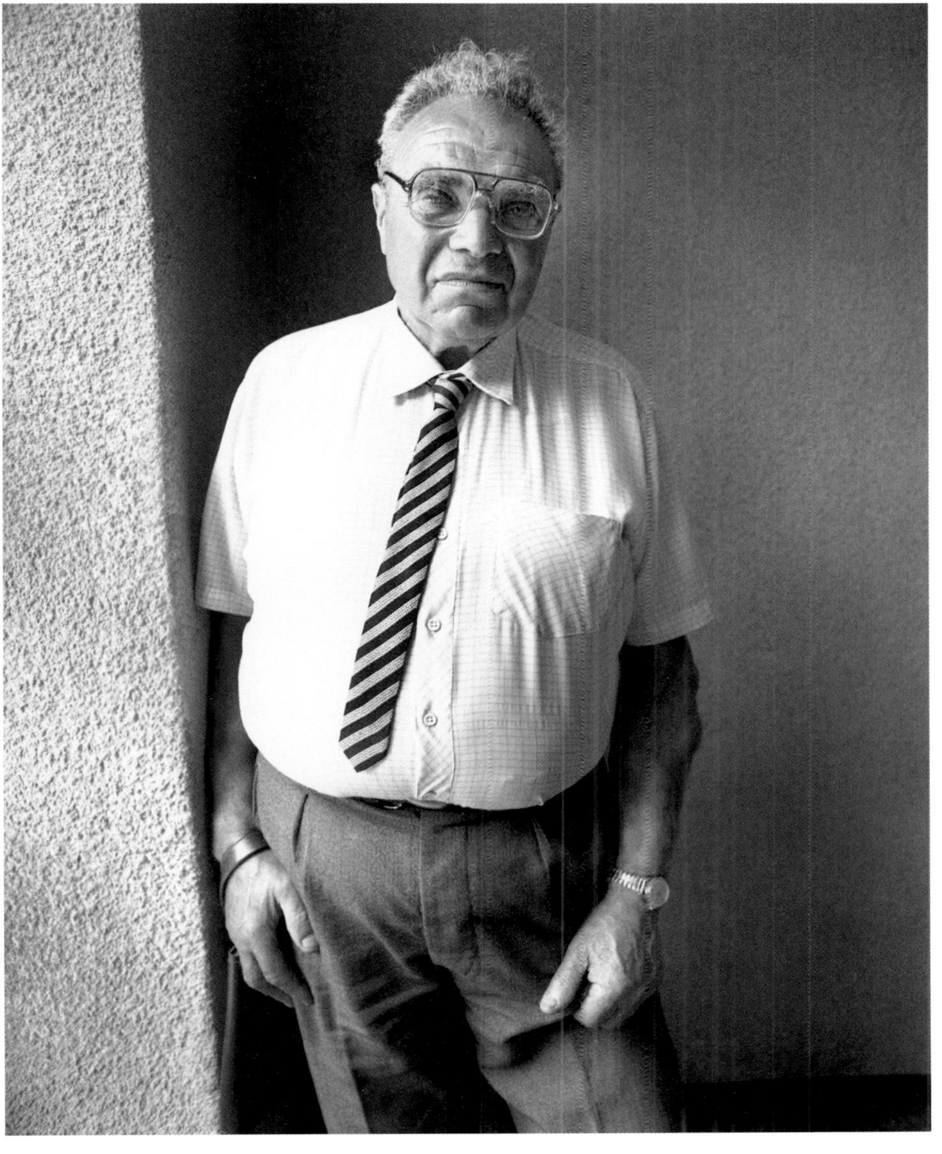

Šmuelis Šragė. Born 1925

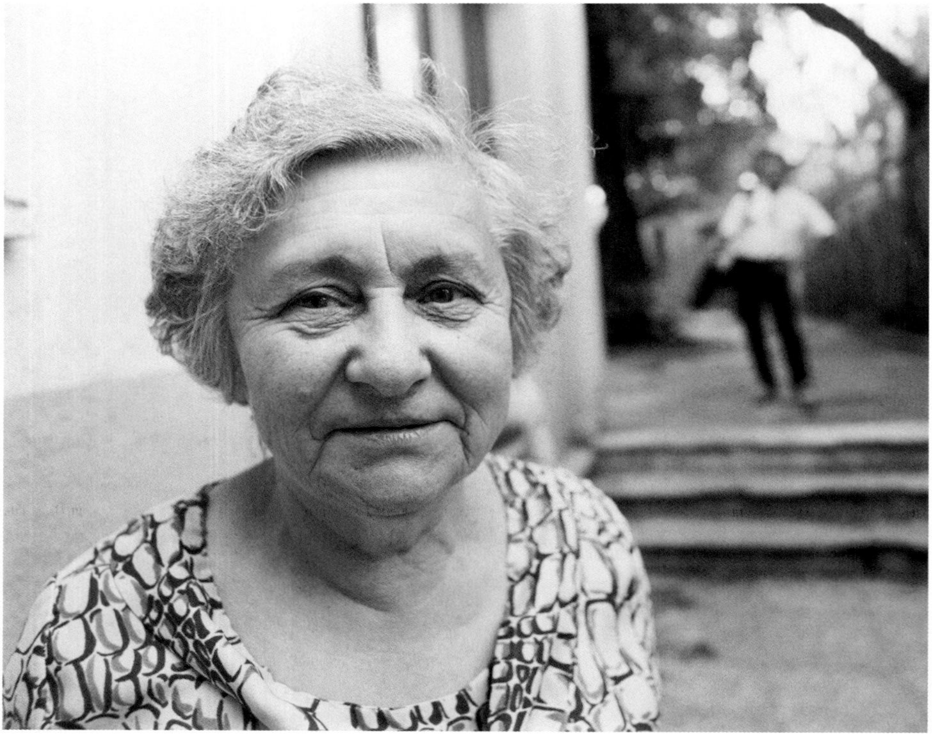

Žene Žimlinskienė. Born 1926

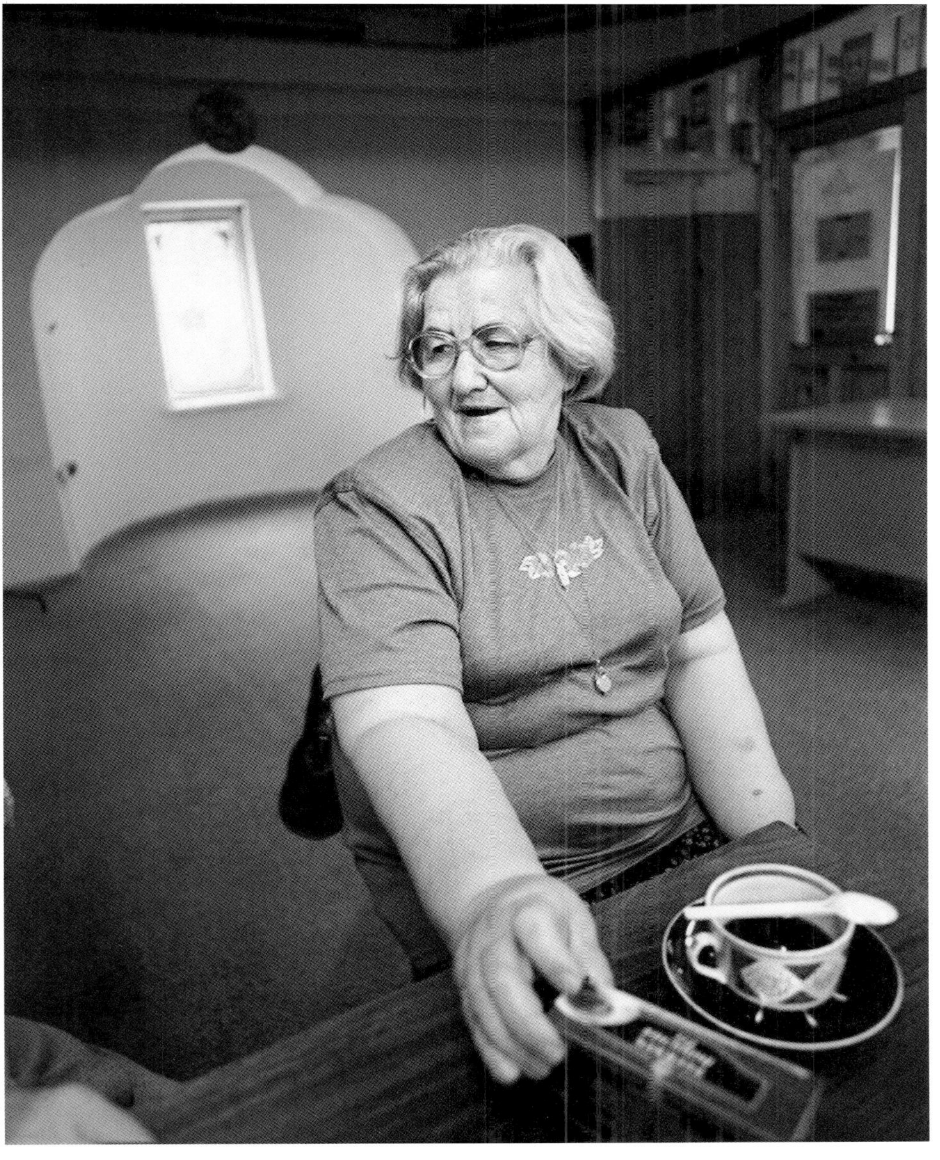

Mirjam Zaborskienė. Born 1923

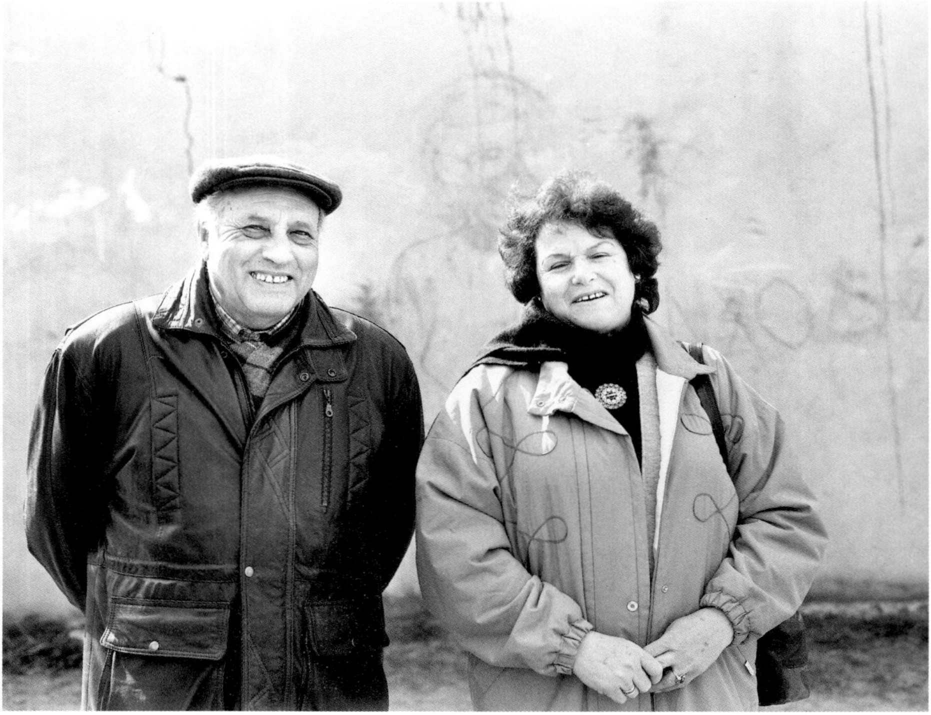

Isaakas Demantas. Born 1929. Mina Fišman. Born 1932

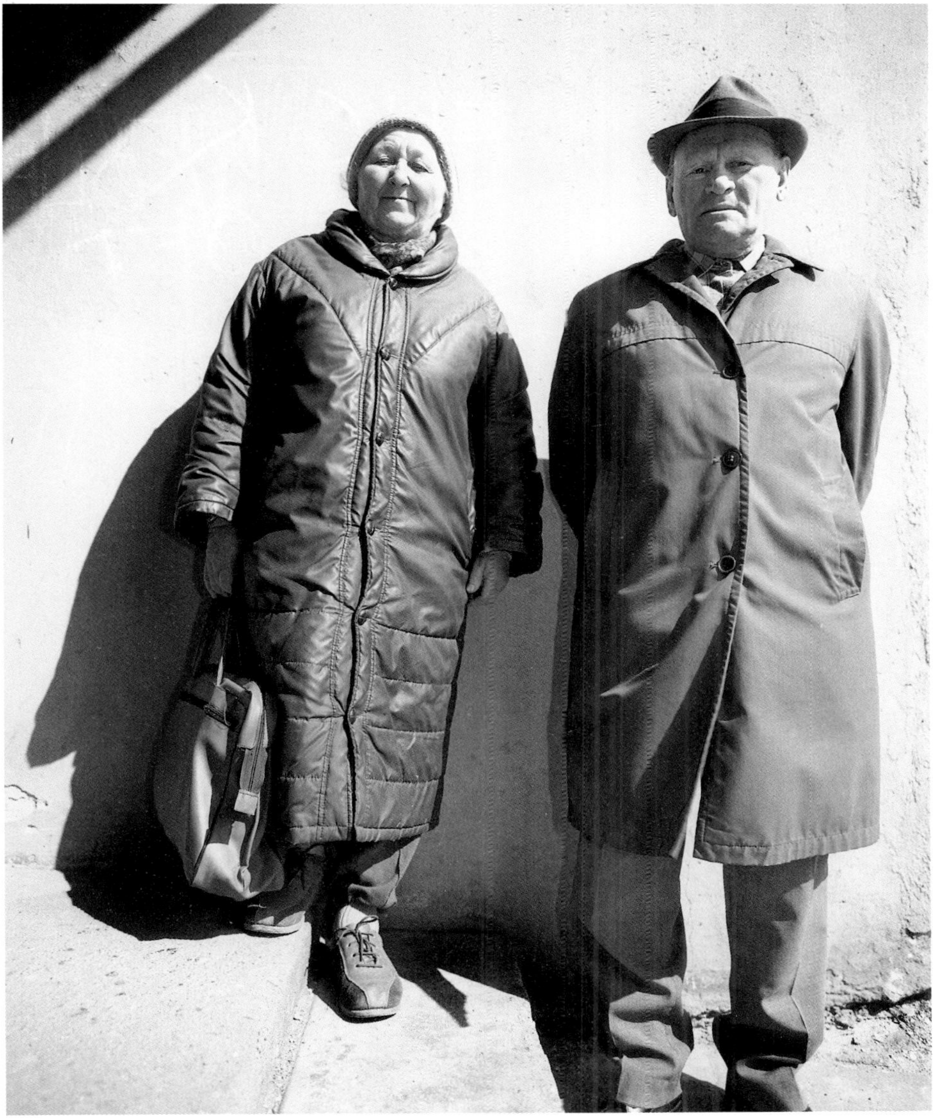

Raja Bastunskienė. Born 1920. Abraomas Bastunskis. Born ˉ919

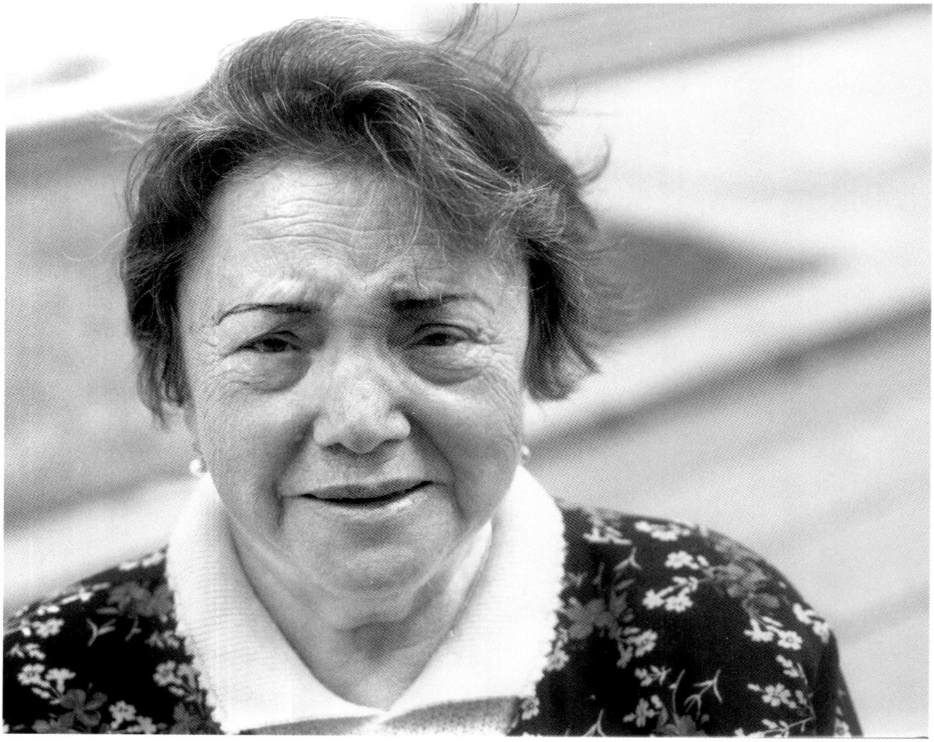

Merė Gotlerytė. Born 1932

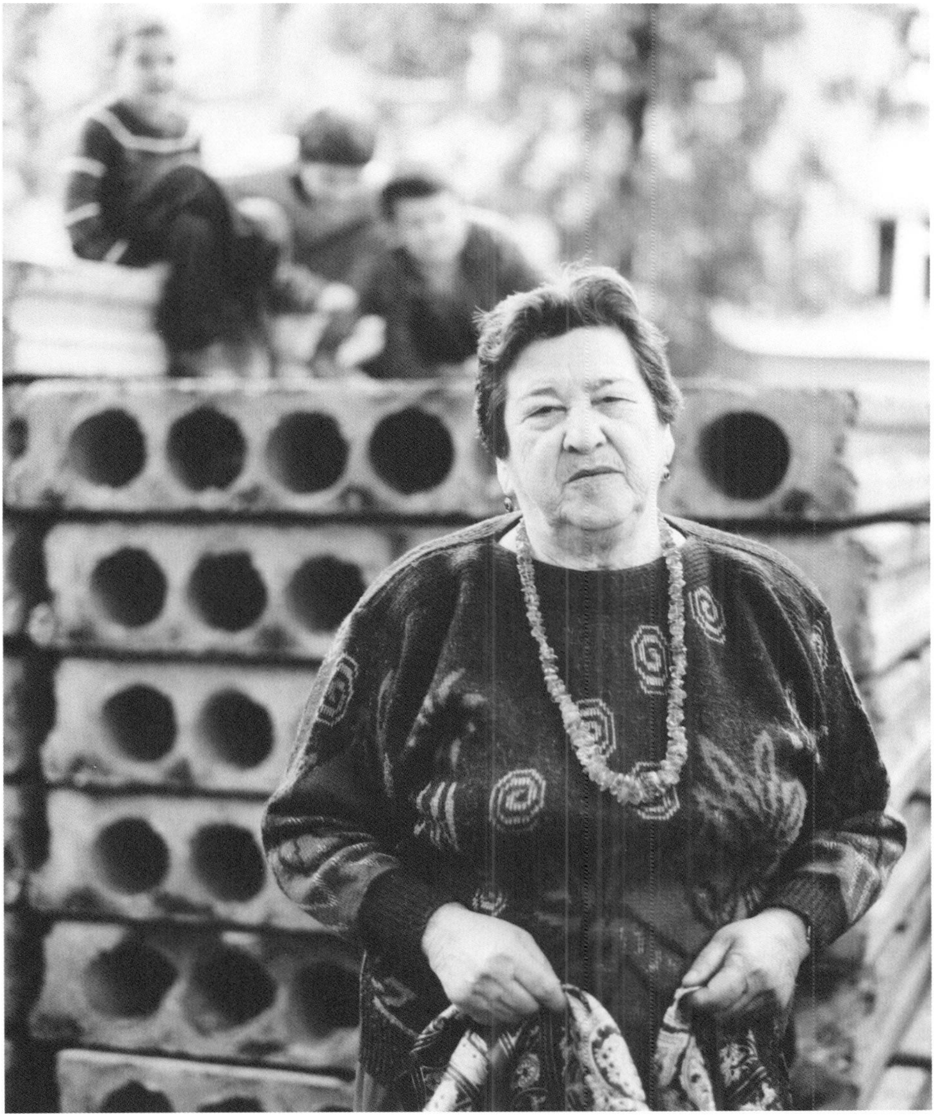

Marija Machnovskaja. Born 1923

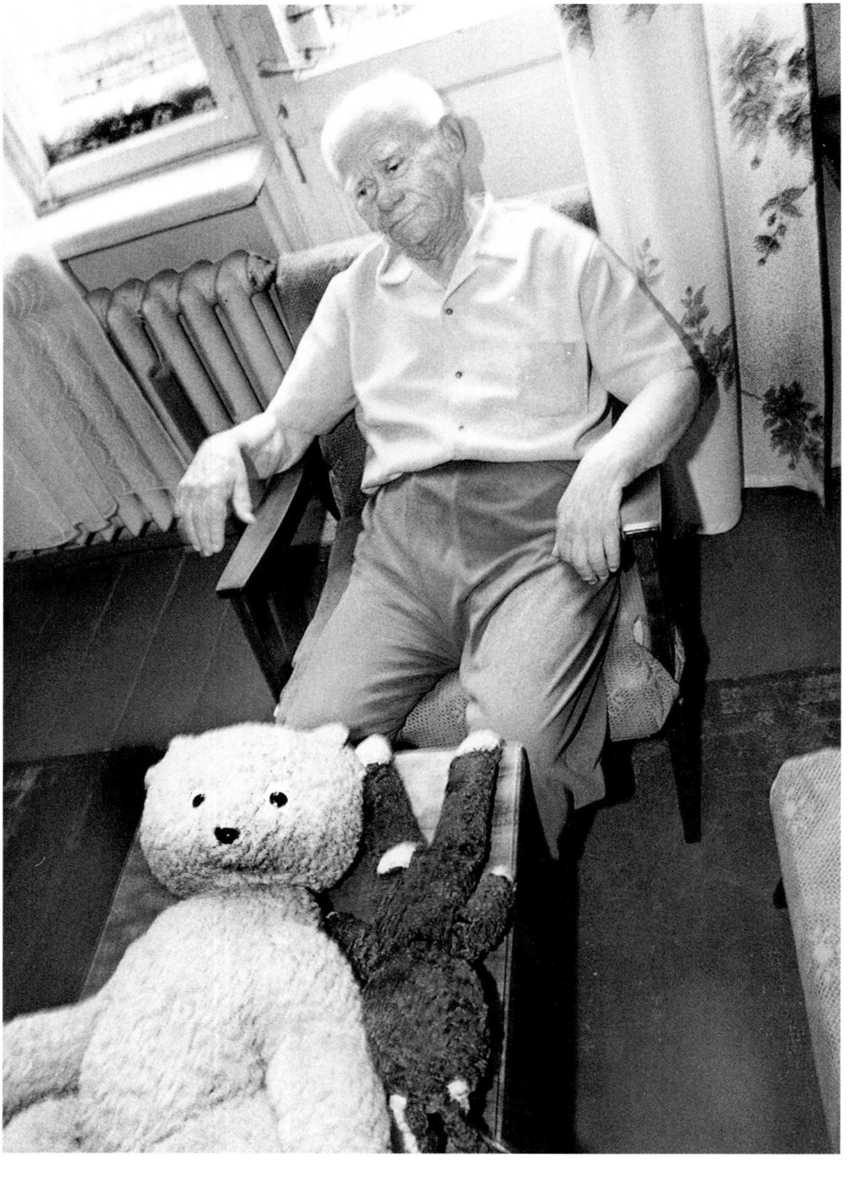

Abraomas Krumas. Born 1908

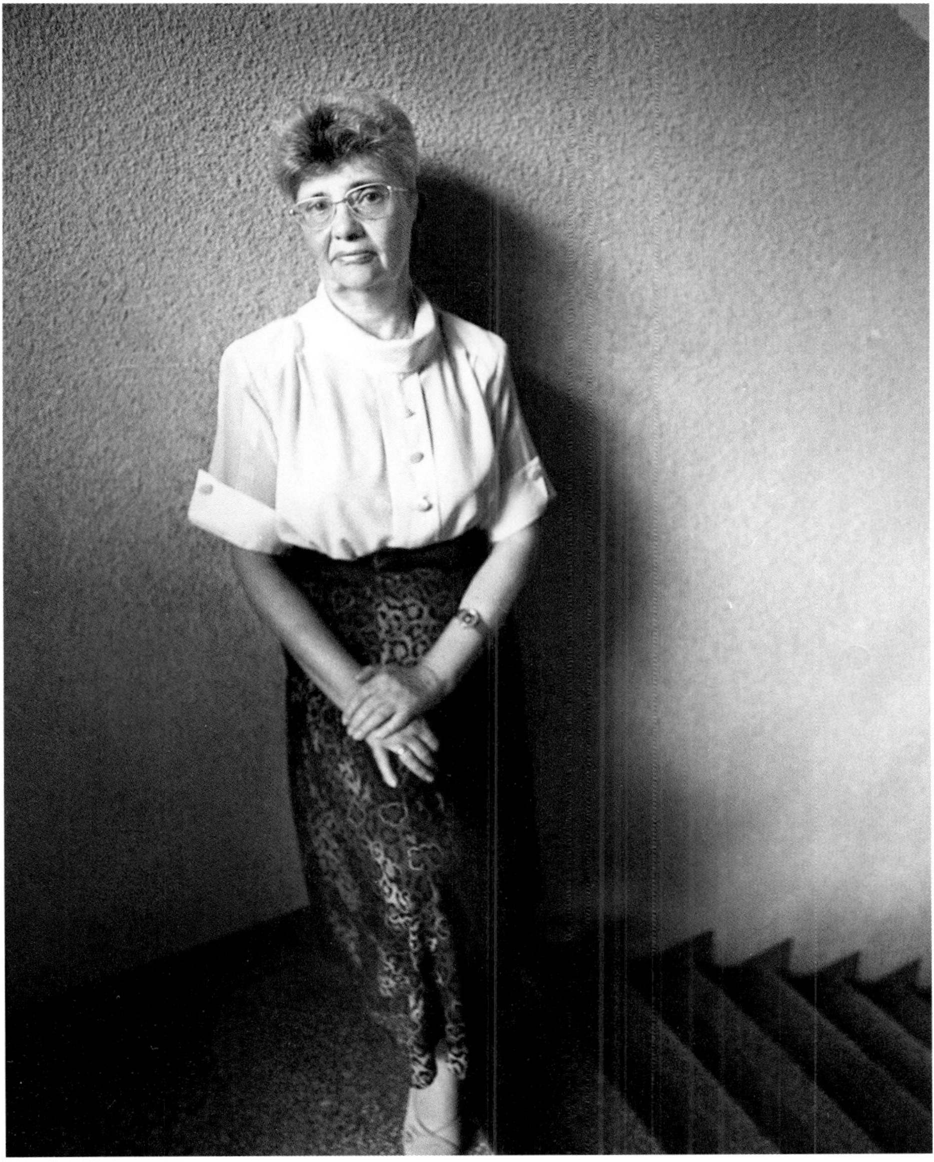

Rūta Noreikienė (Liuba Milerytė). Born 1940

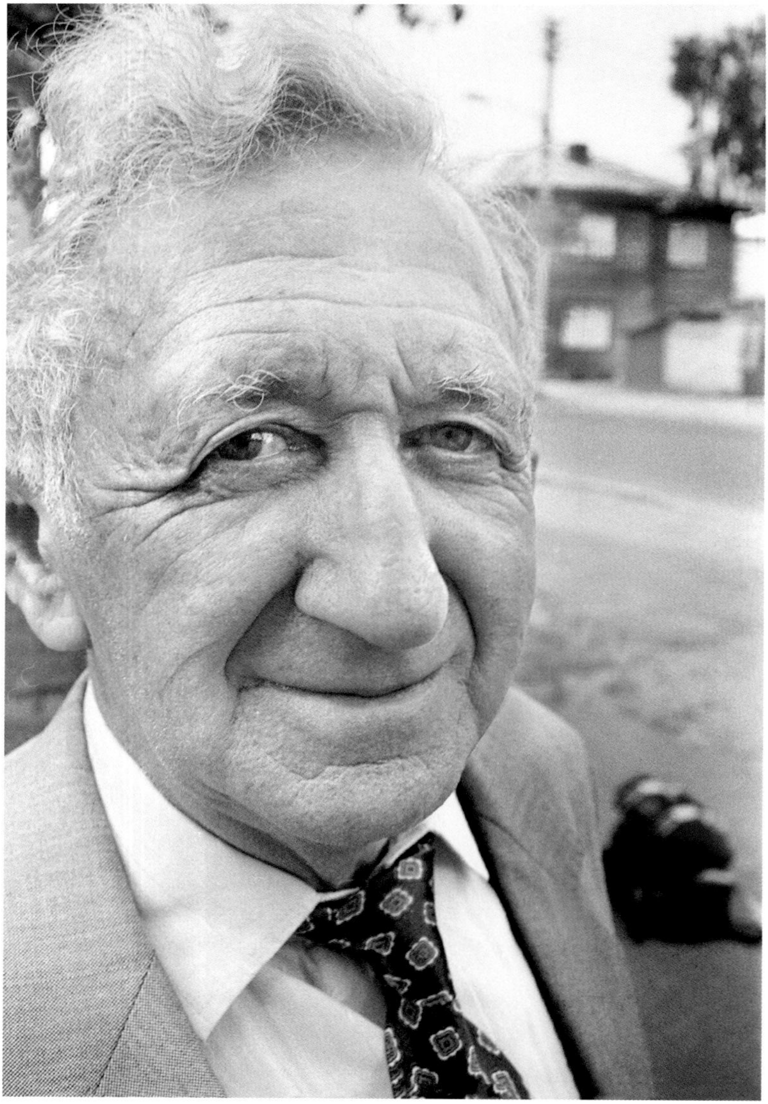

Davis Sasover. Born 1926

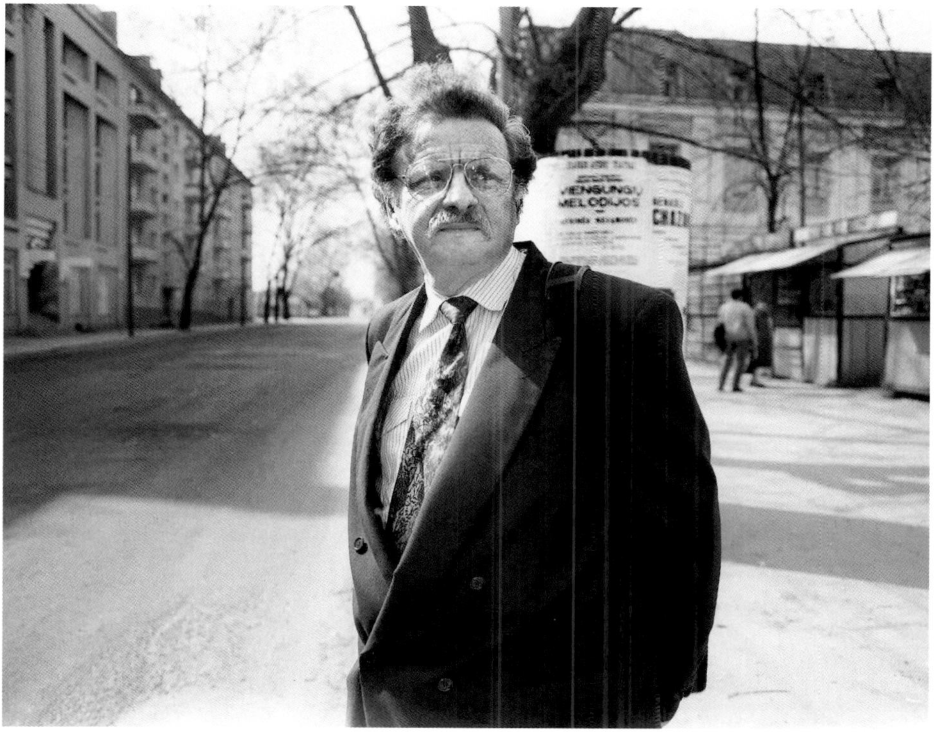

Faivelis Galpernas. Born 1929

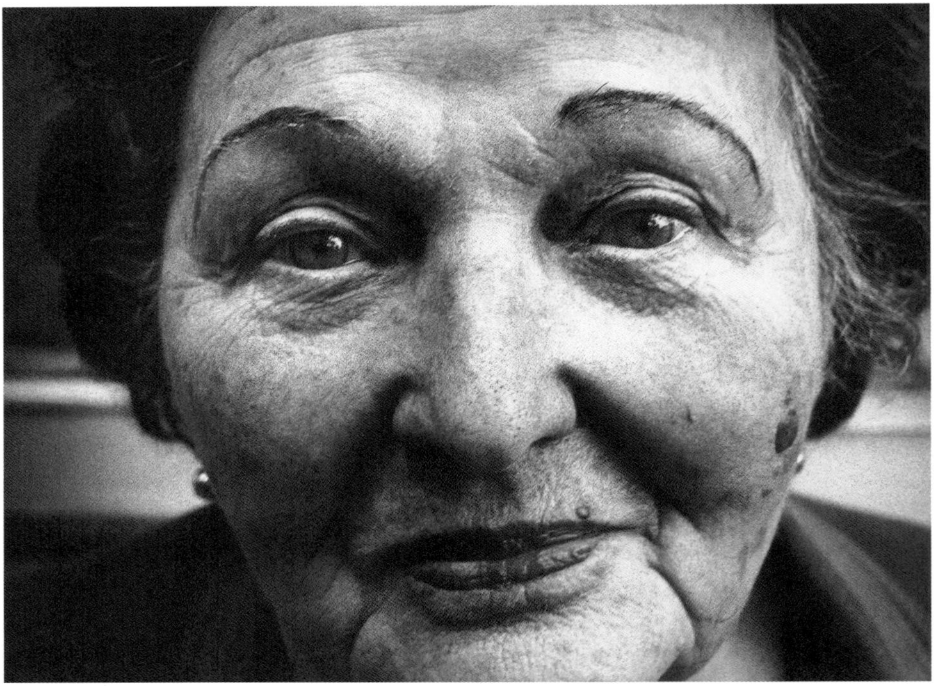

Klara Černiauskienė. Born 1917

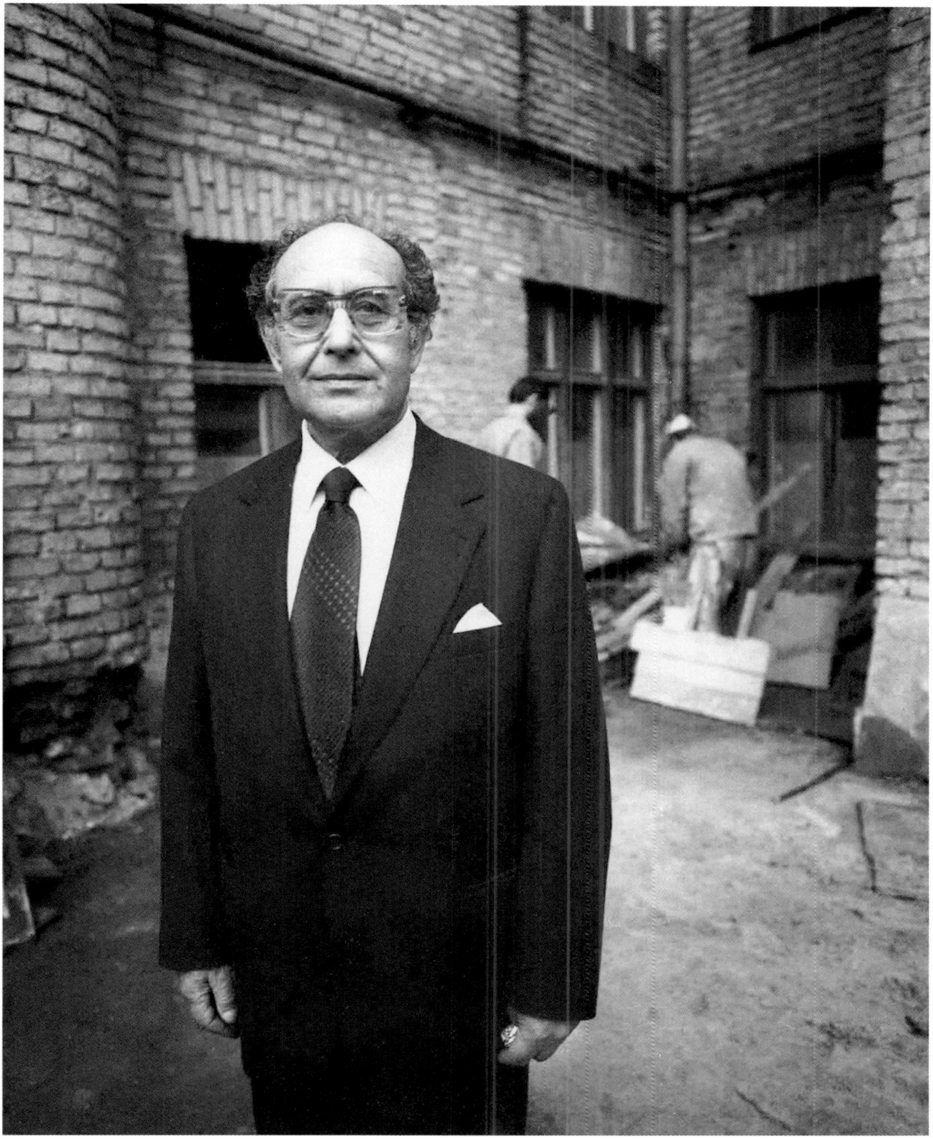

Tobijas Jafetas. Born 1930

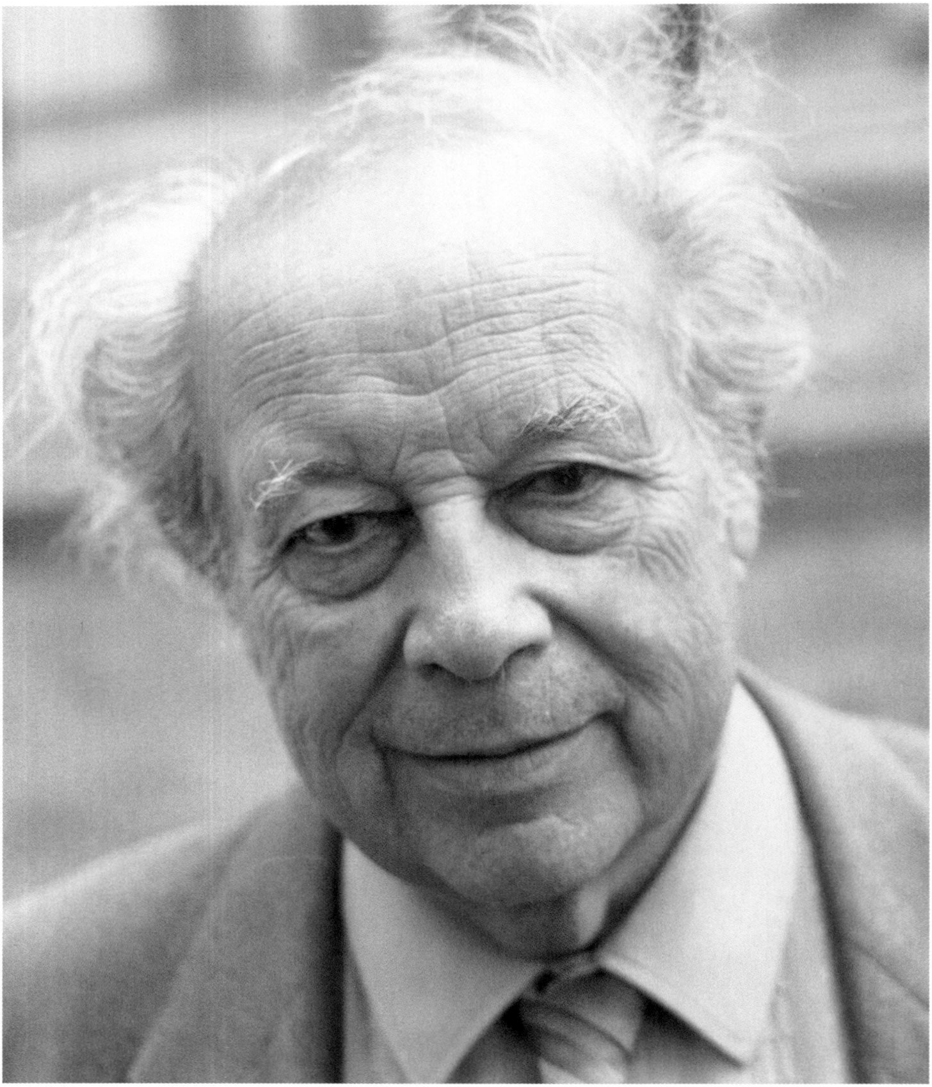

Eduardas Gutmanas. Born 1923

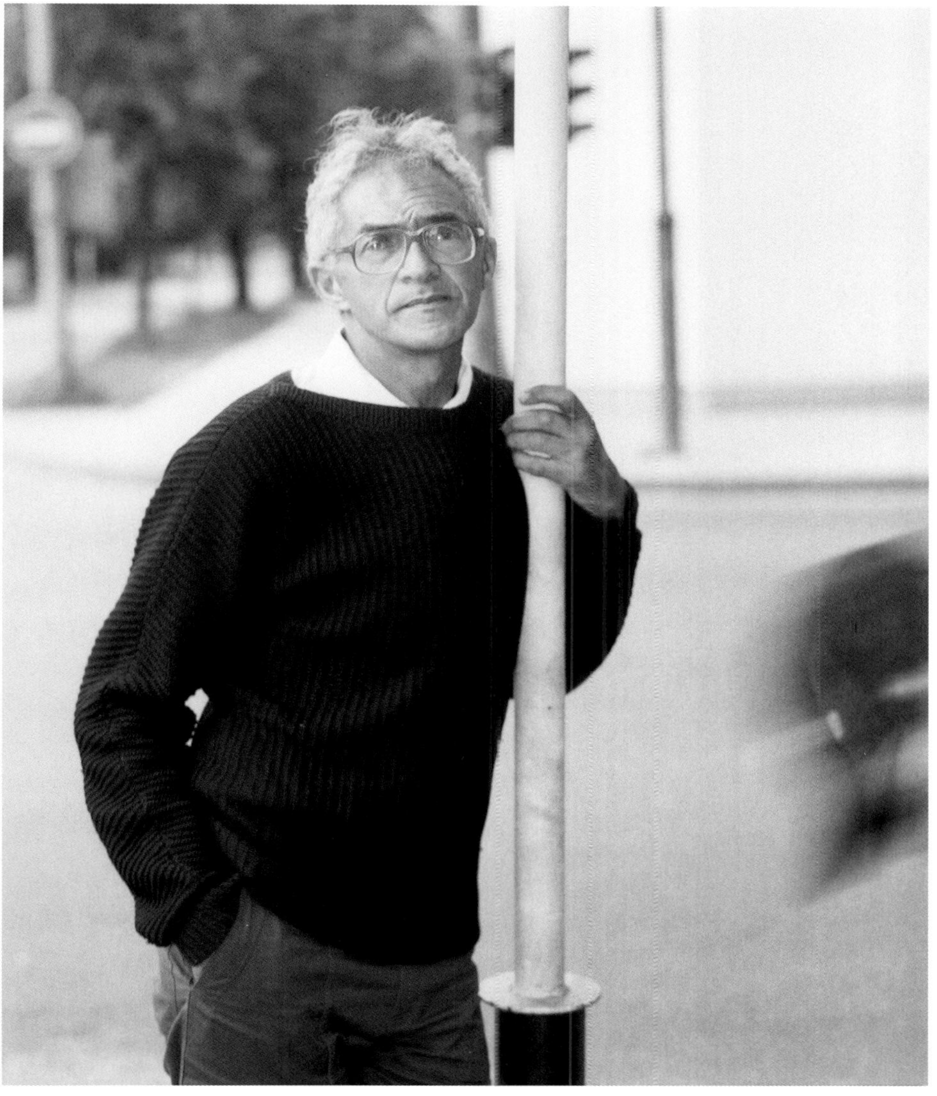

Dovydas Leibnicas. Born 1920

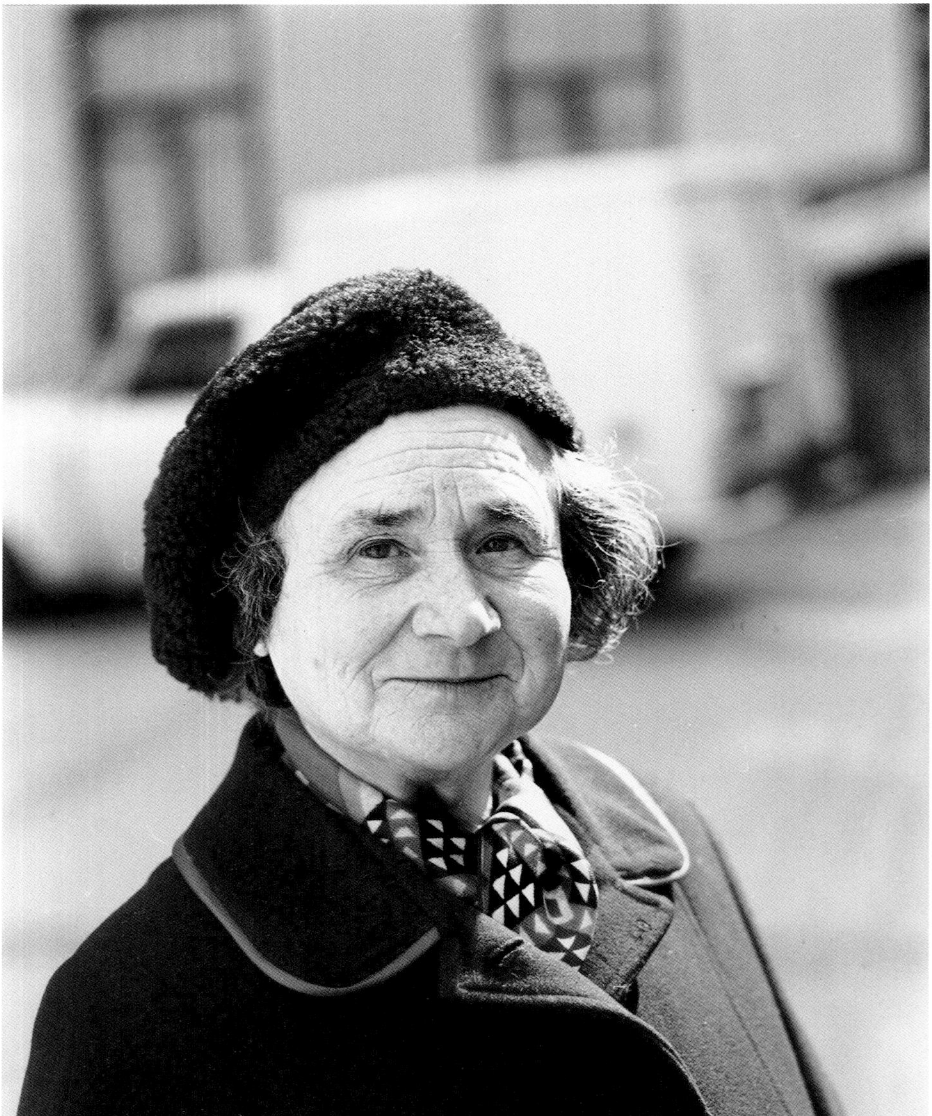

Sulamit Gelpern. Born 1926

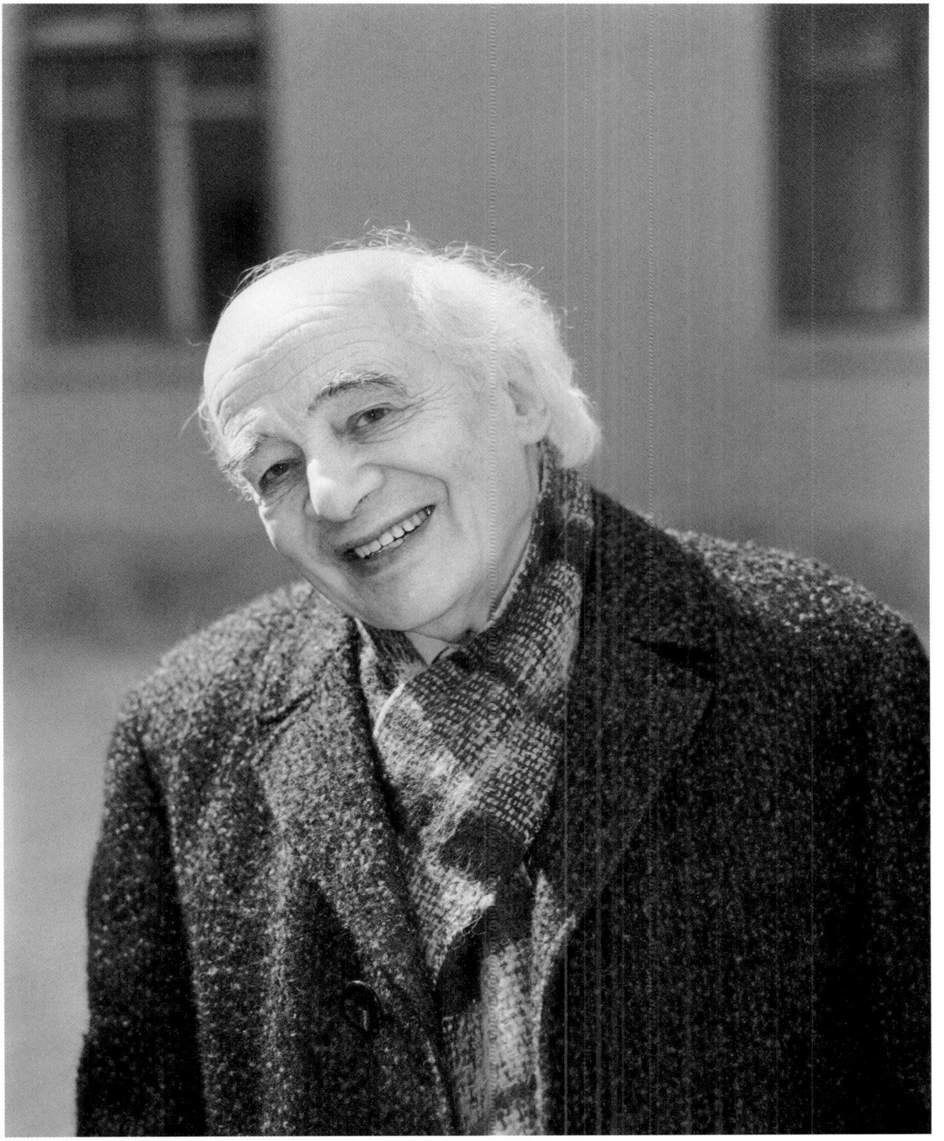

Dmitrijus Gelpernas. Born 1914

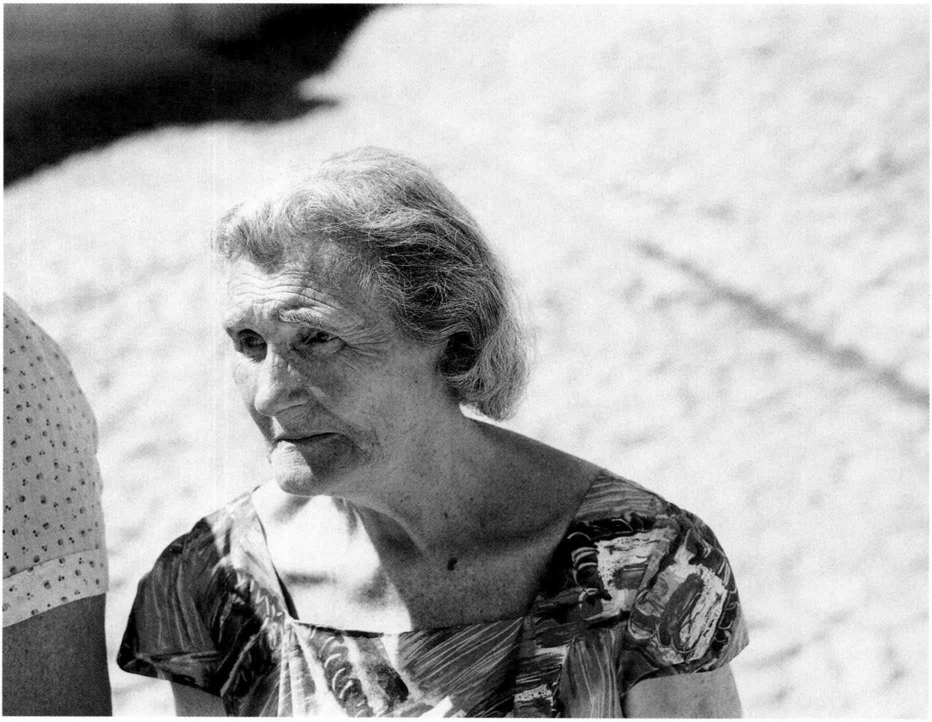

Commemoration meeting to mark the 50th anniversary of the liquidation of the Kaunas ghetto. 1994

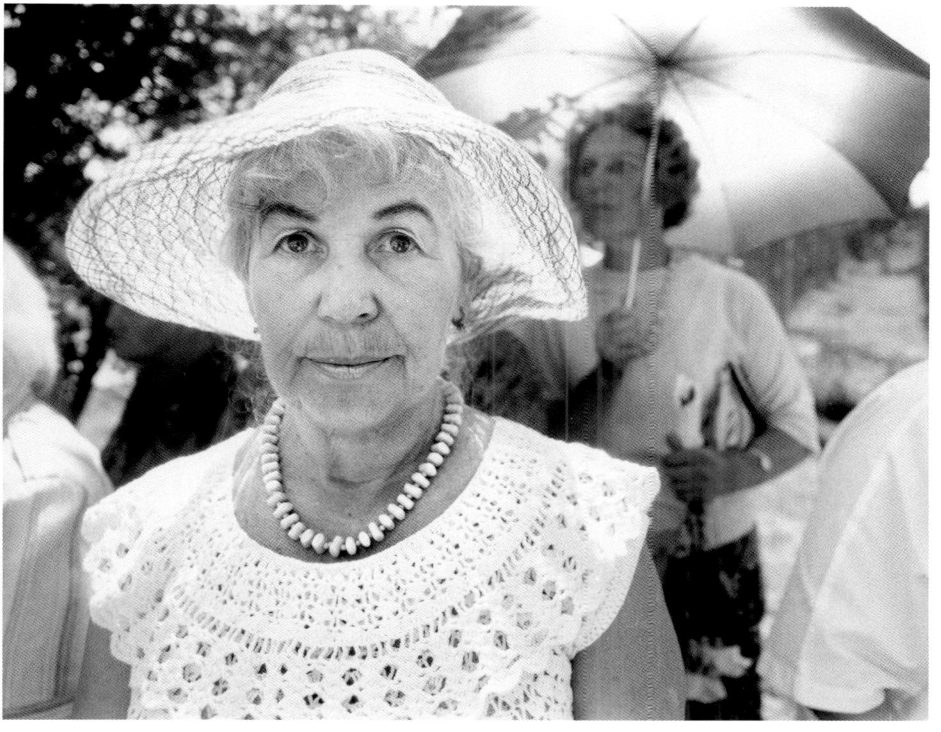

Commemoration meeting to mark the 50th anniversary of the liquidation of the Kaunas ghetto. 1994

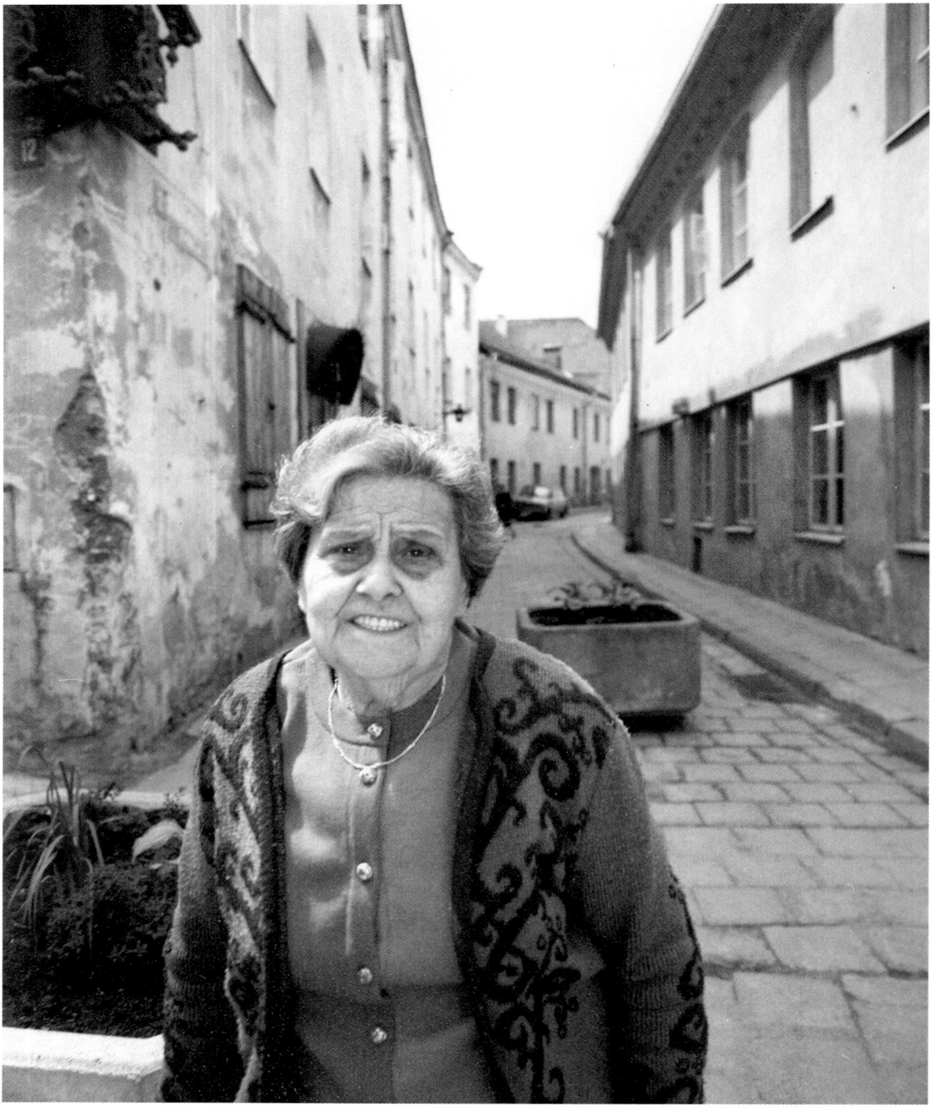

Keilė Kaplan. Born 1912

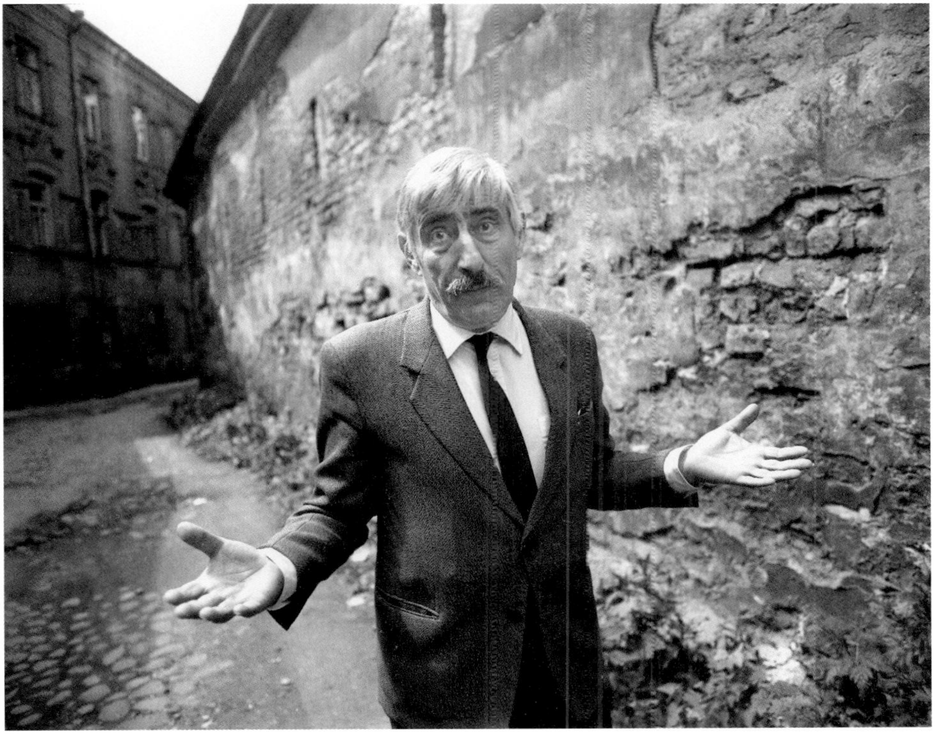

Dmitrijus Kopelmanas. Born 1927

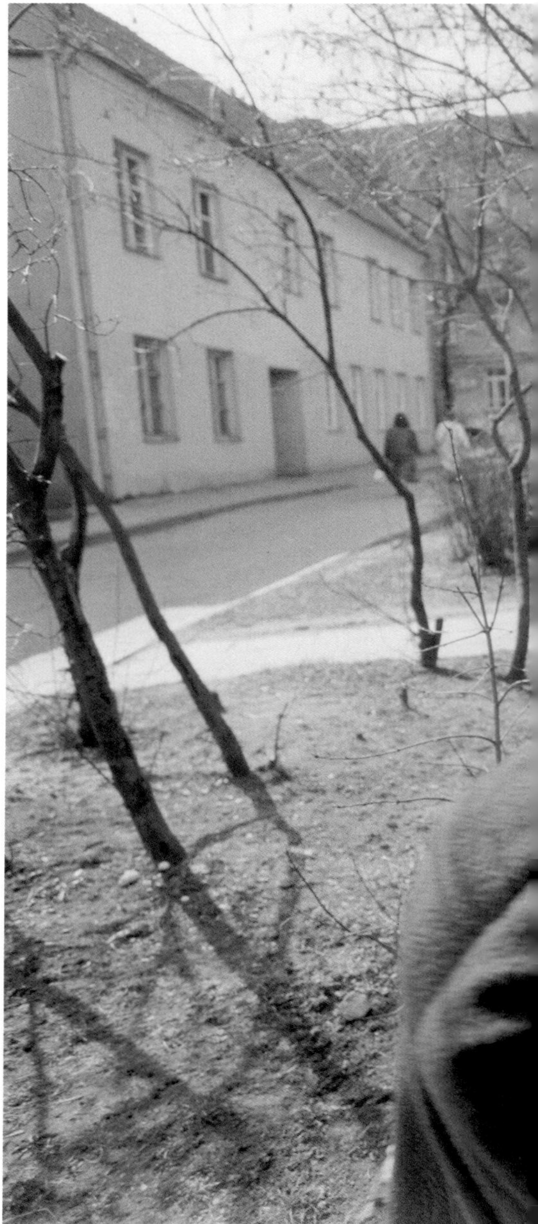

Isaakas Demantas. Born 1929

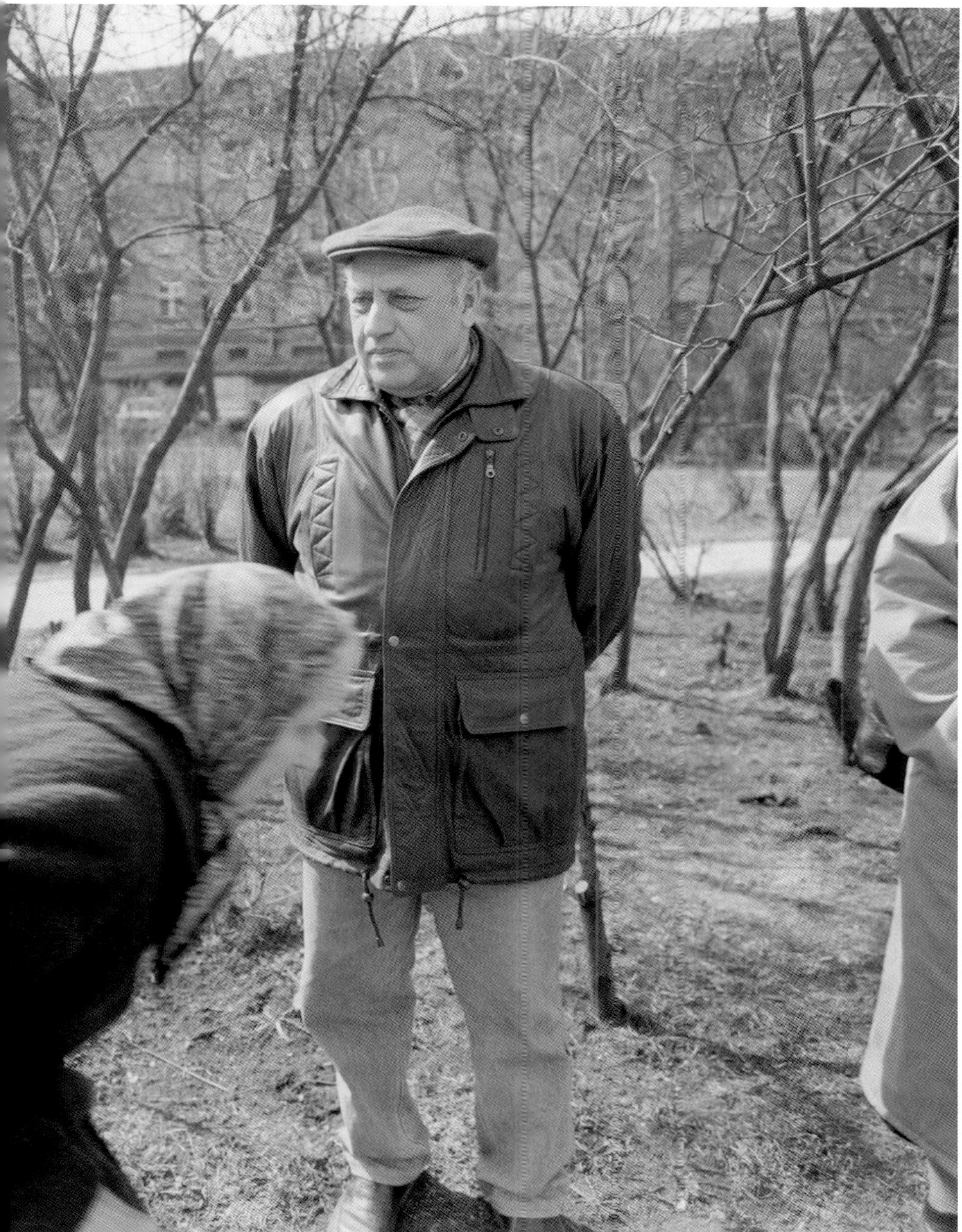

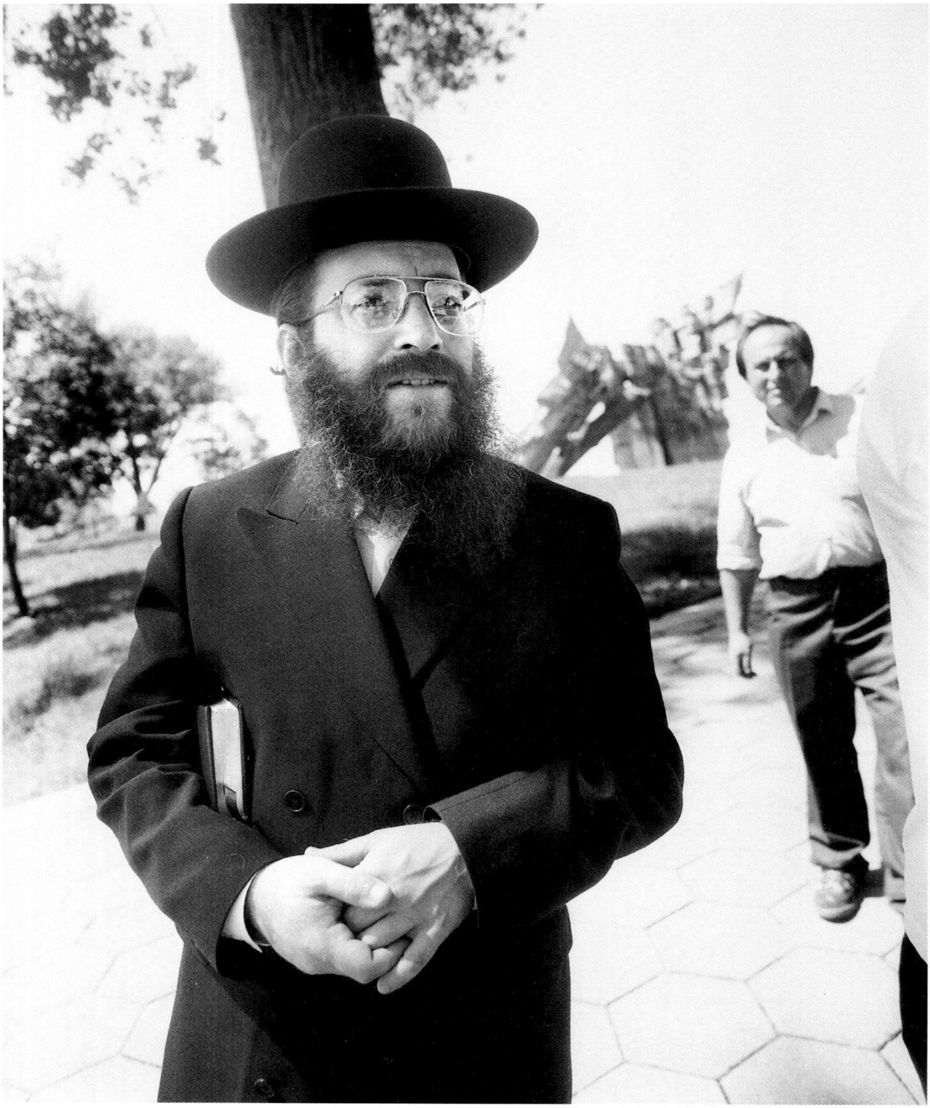

Commemoration meeting to mark the 50th anniversary
of the liquidation of the Kaunas ghetto. 1994

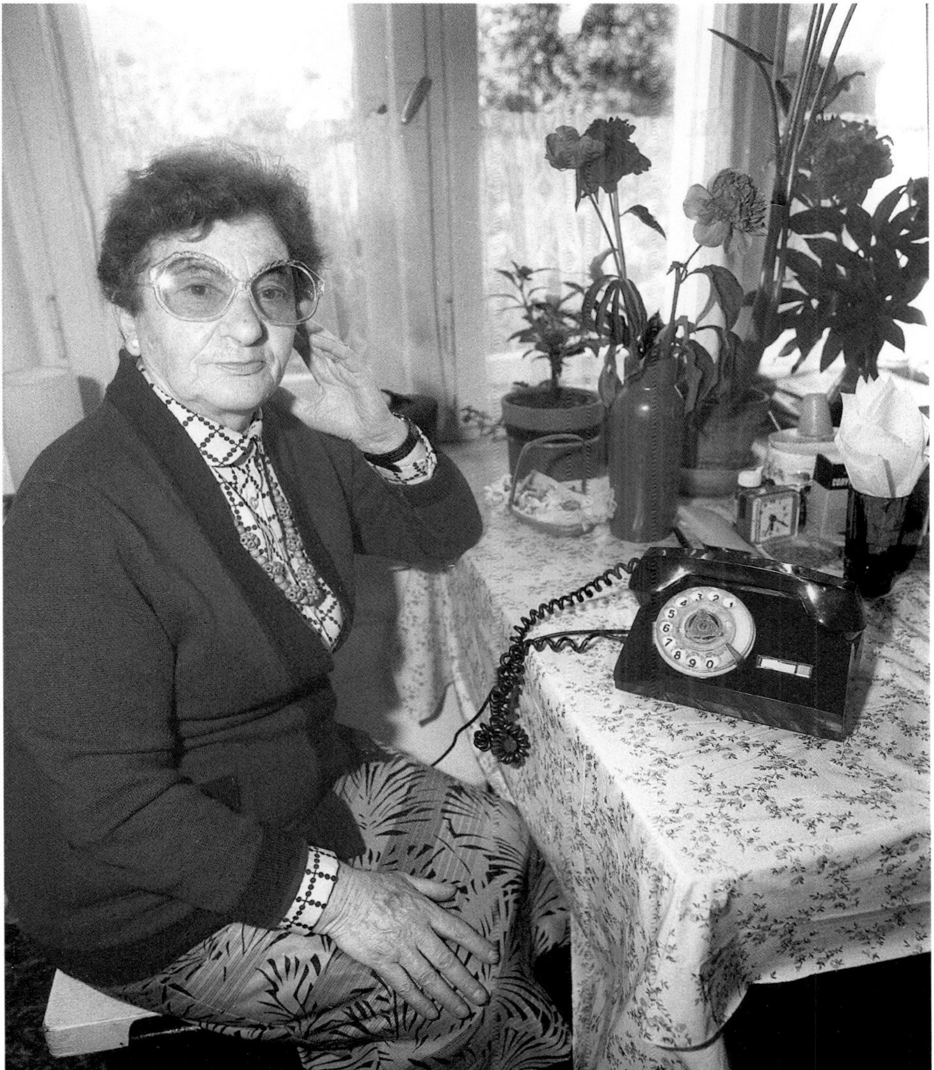

Lėja Finkelšteinaitė. Born 1919

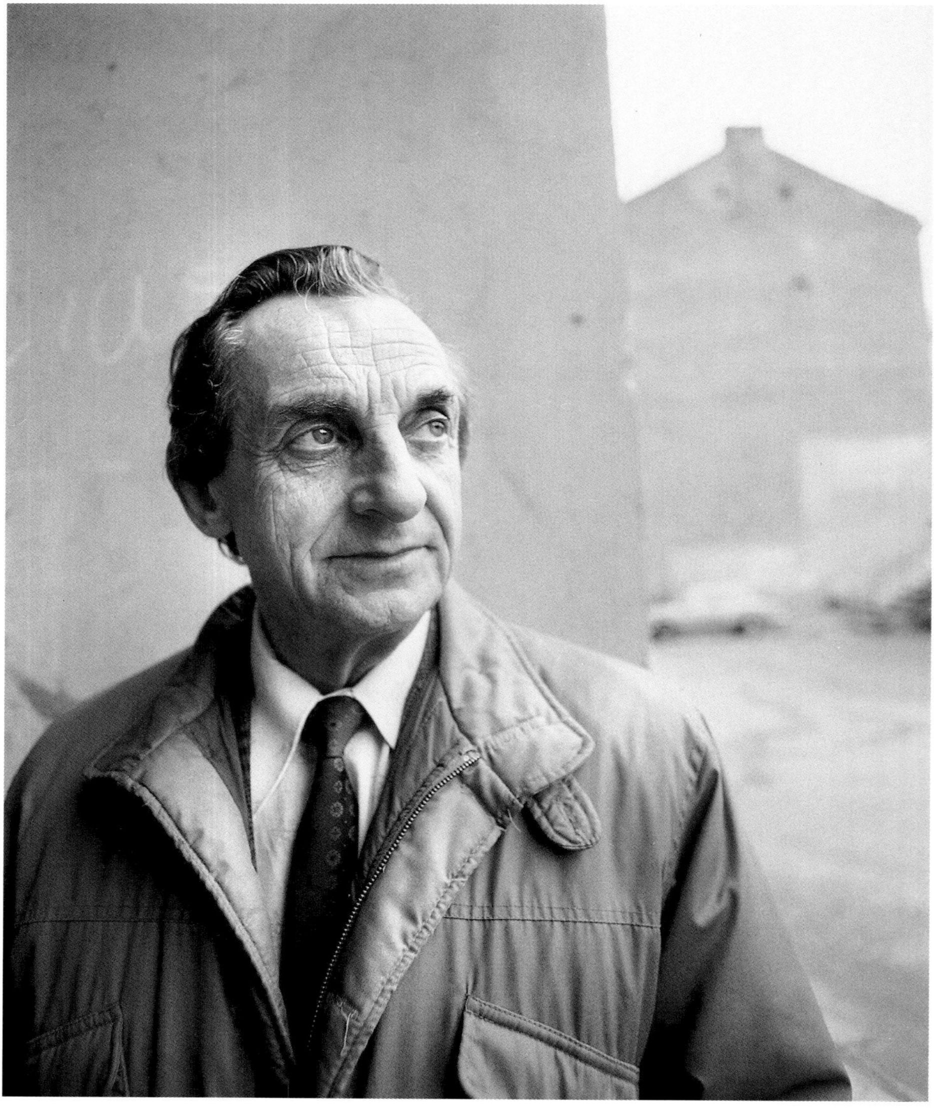

Chaimas Glikas. Born 1924

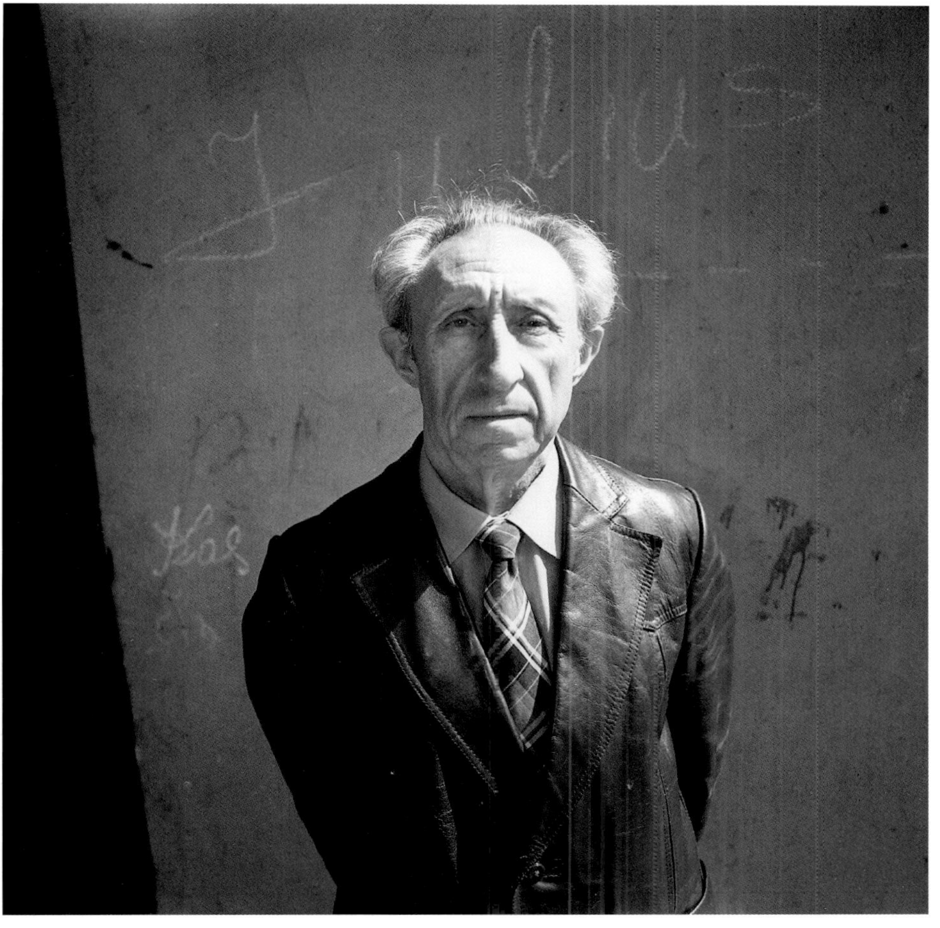

Gedalija Kremeris. Born 1930

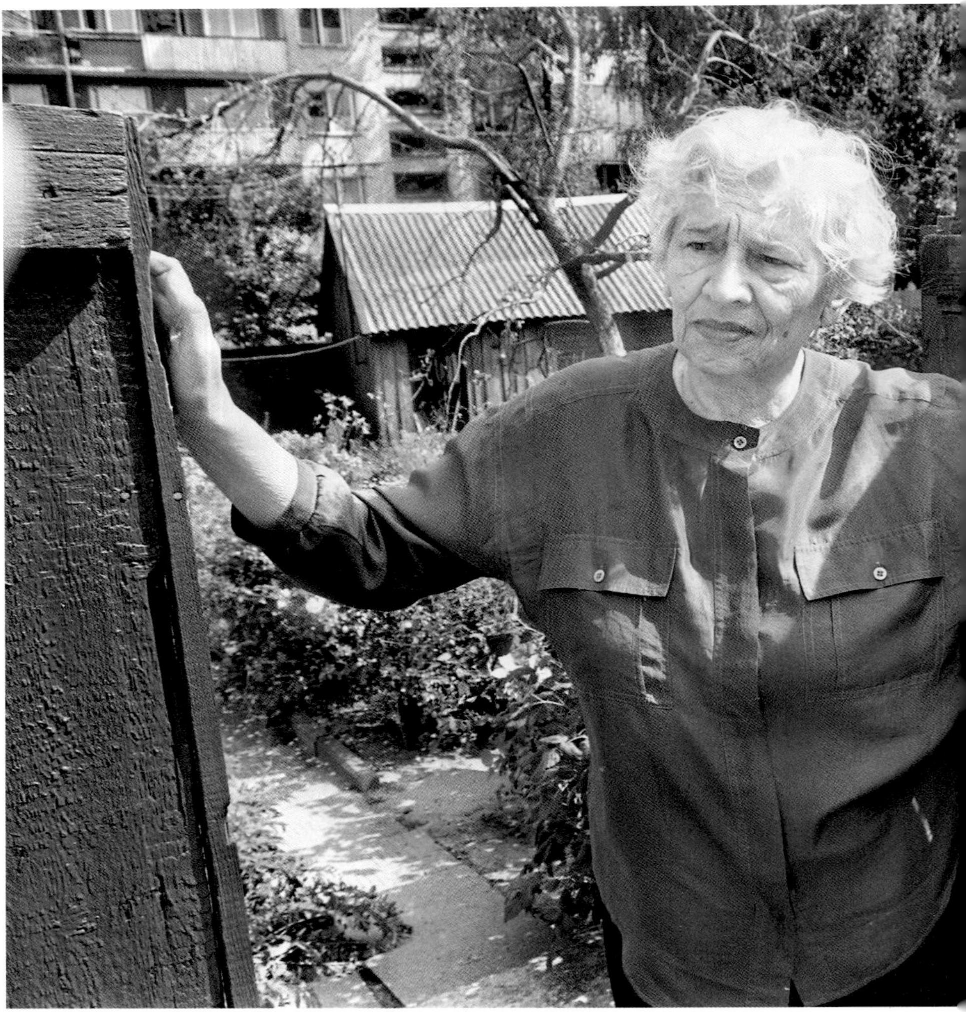

Jocheved Inčiūrienė. Born 1924

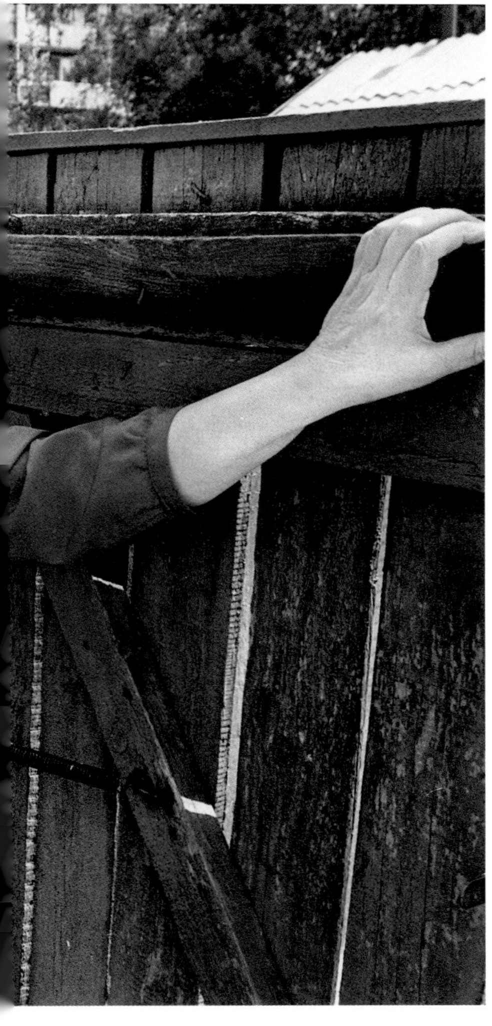

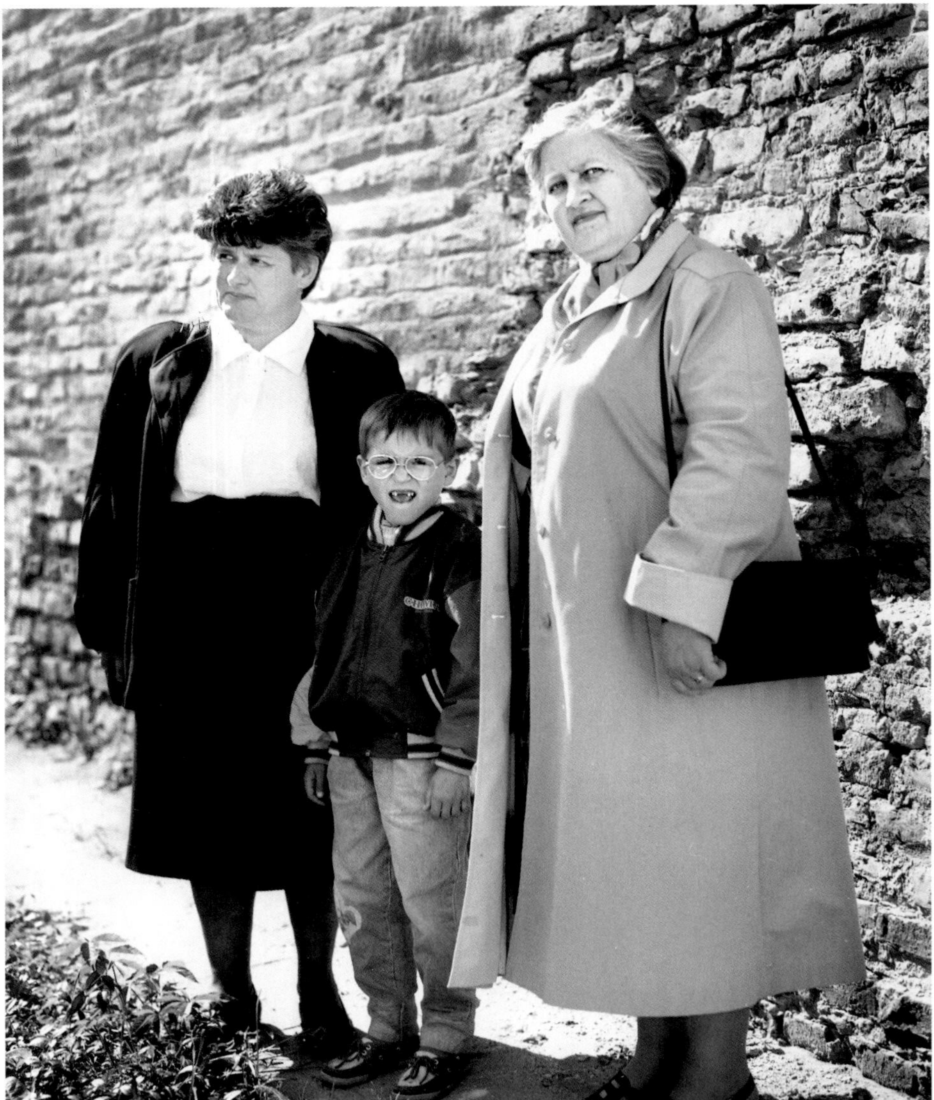

Liudmila Tarasenkova. Born 1942. Bliuma Taločkienė. Born 1934

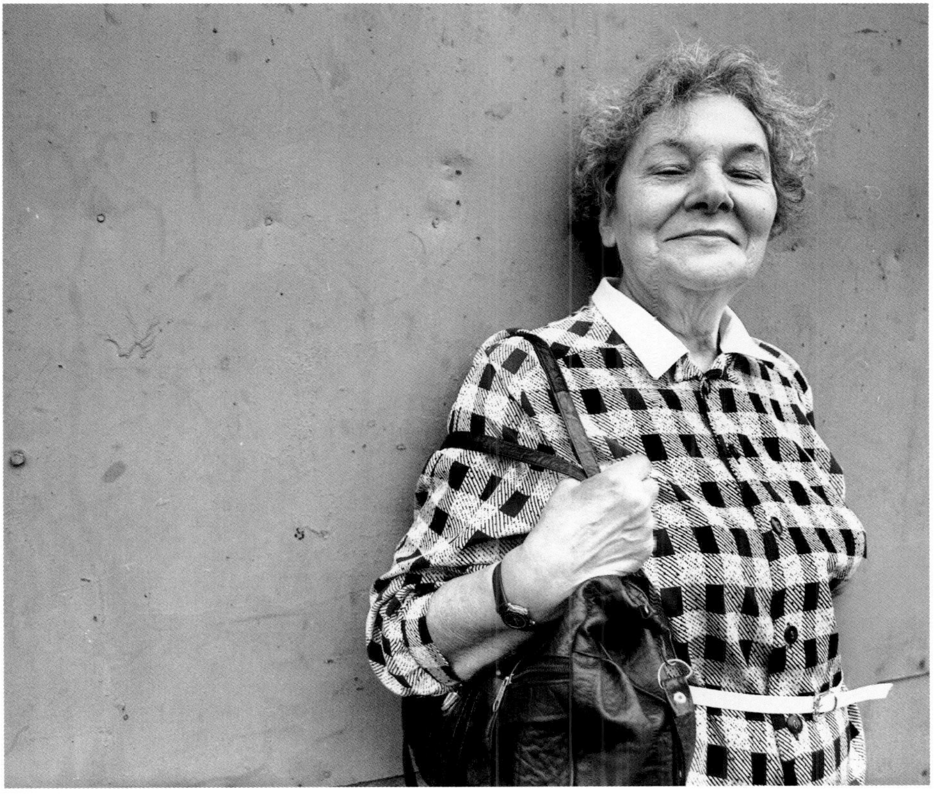

Polina Zingerienė. Born 1922

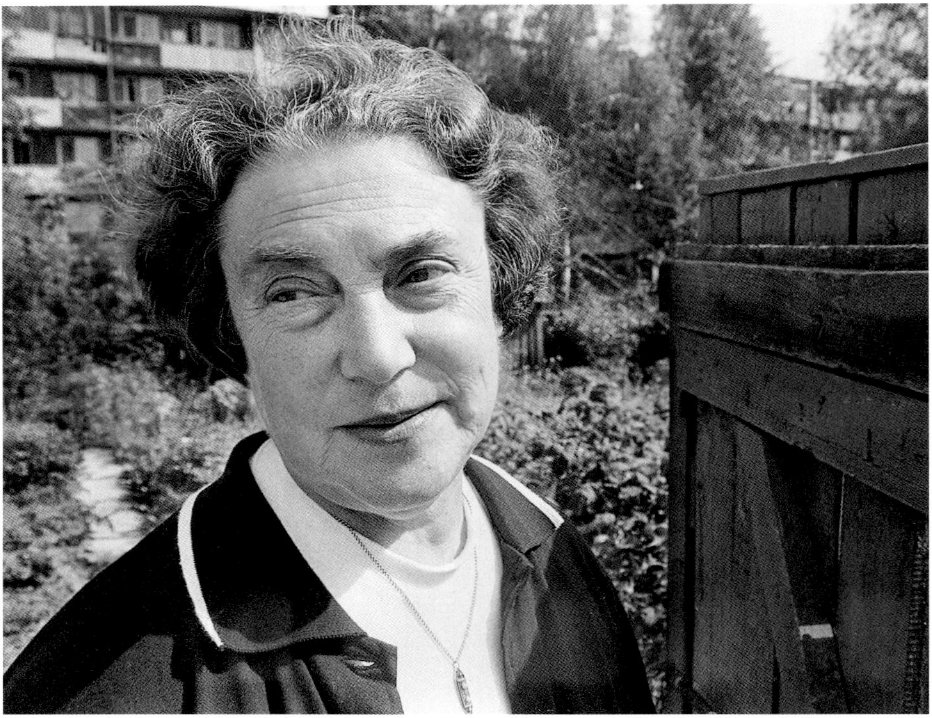

Frumė Kučinskienė. Born 1933

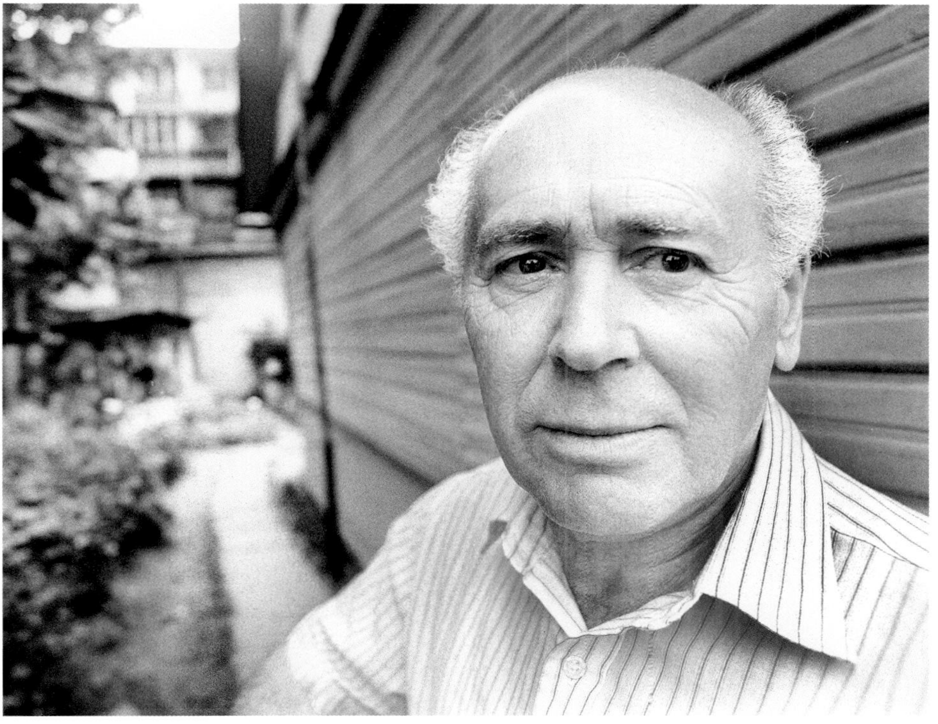

Mejeris Kujavskis. Born 1925

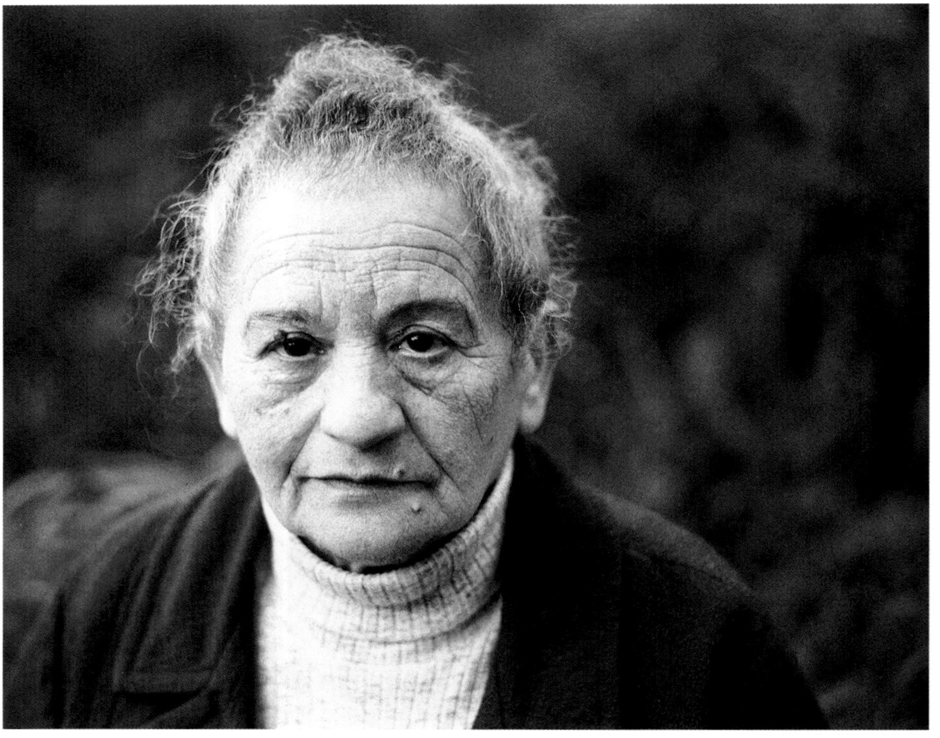

Merė Klaz. Born 1918

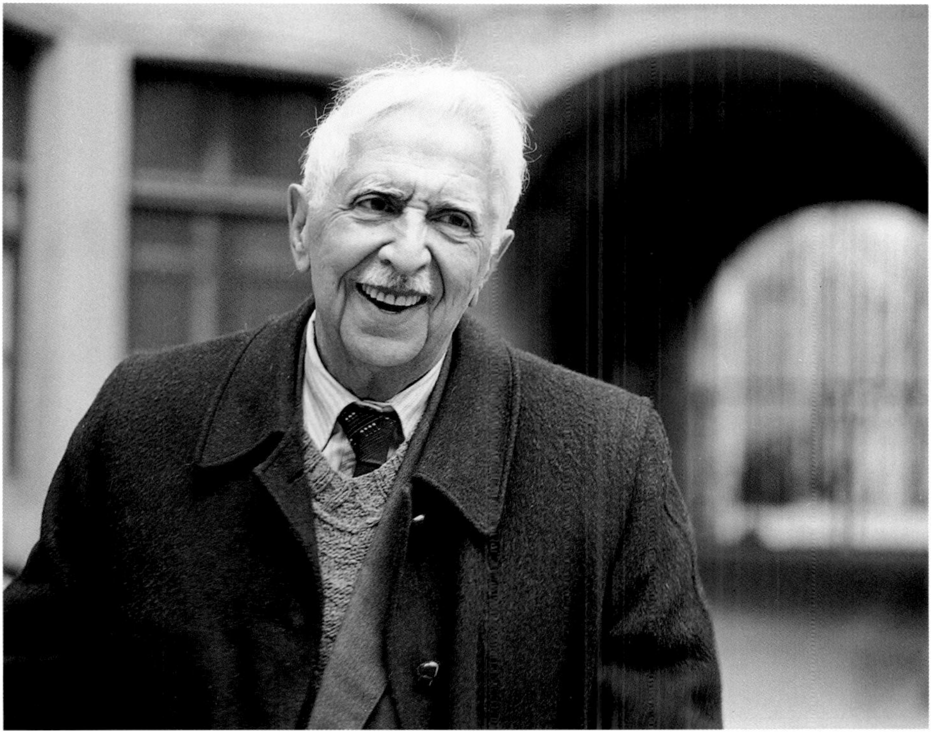

Benjaminas Cvizonas. Born 1922

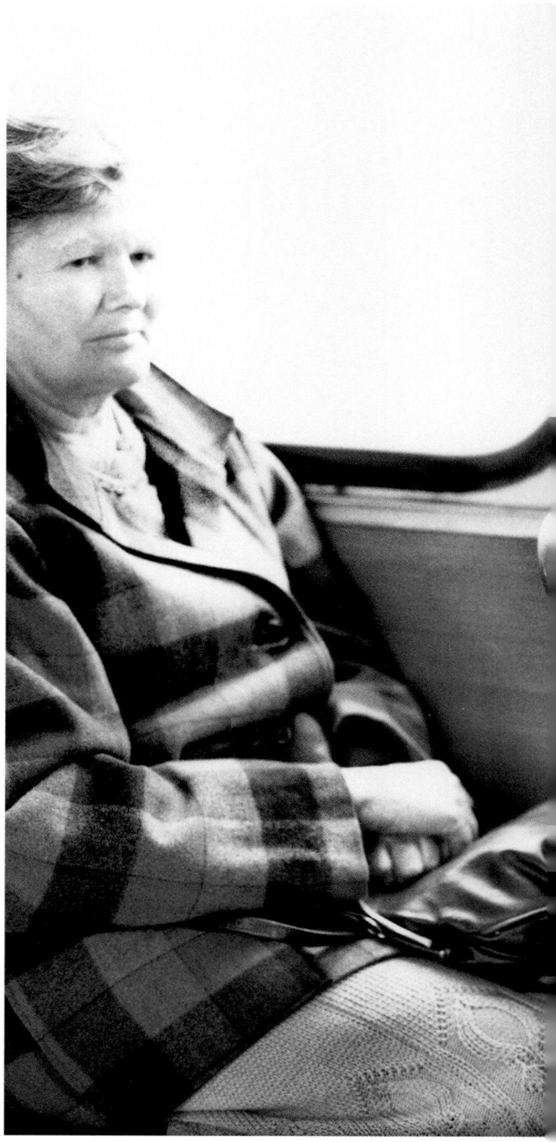

Šeina Lupšicienė. Born 1922

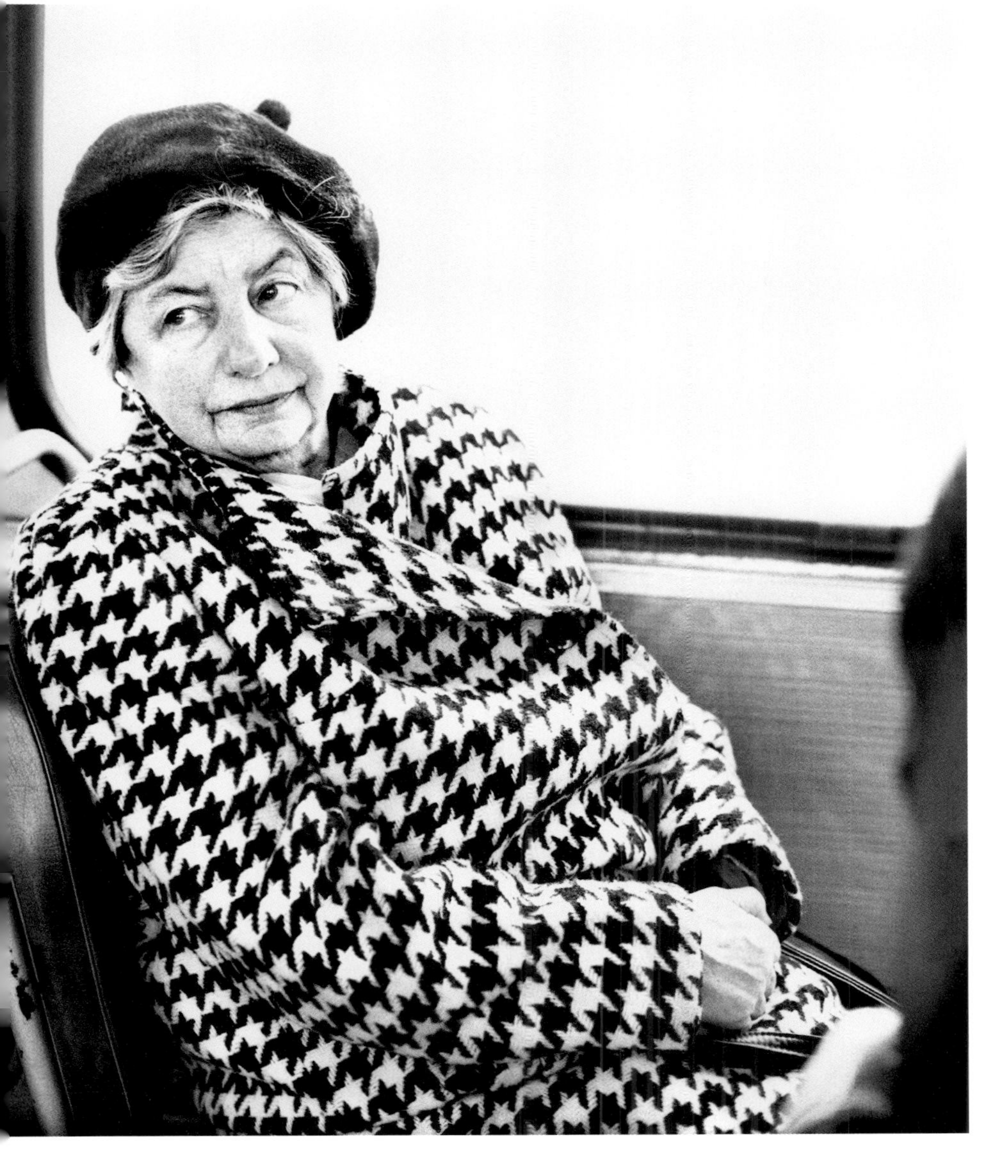

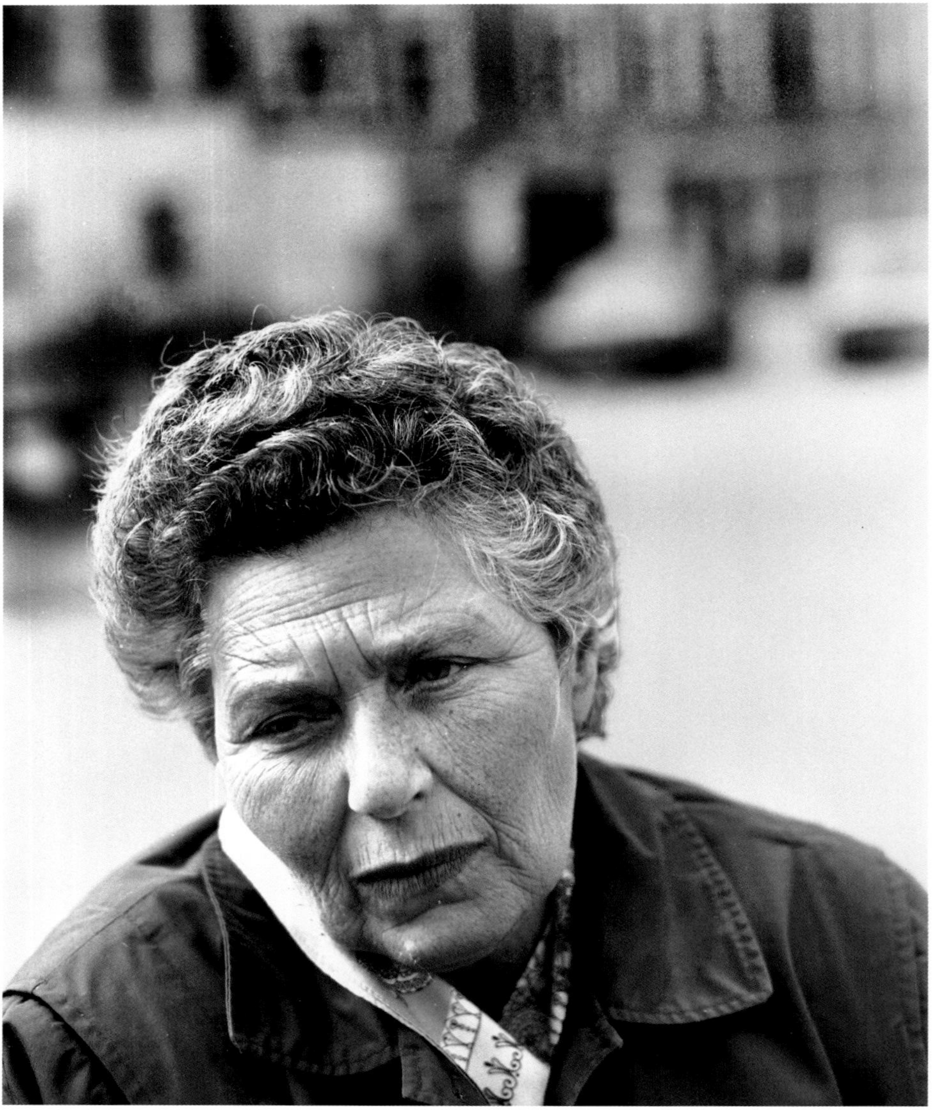

Eta Černova. Born 1928

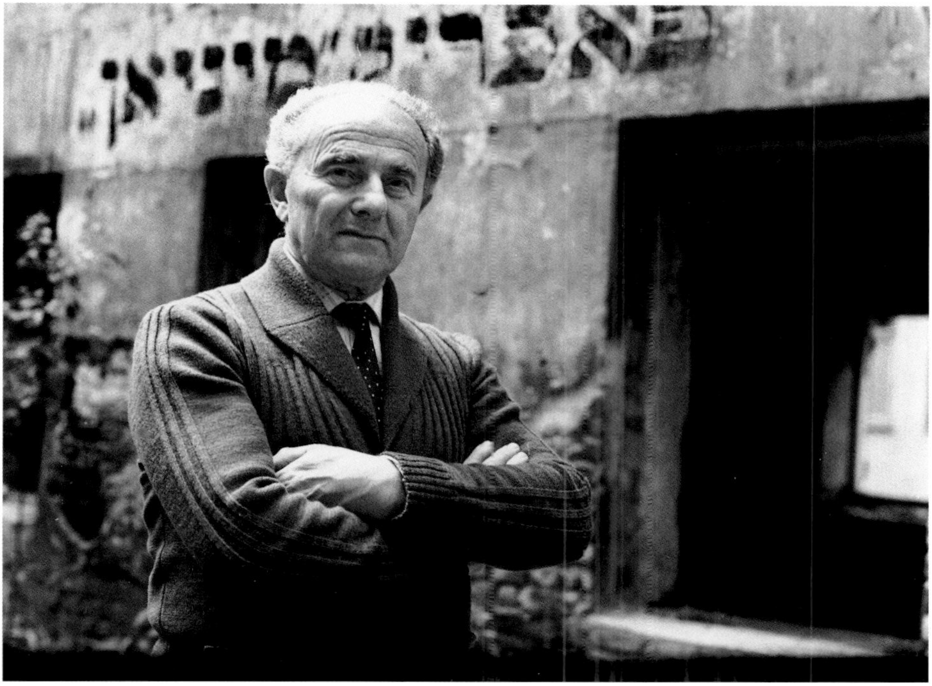

Grigorijus Kaševskis. Born 1936

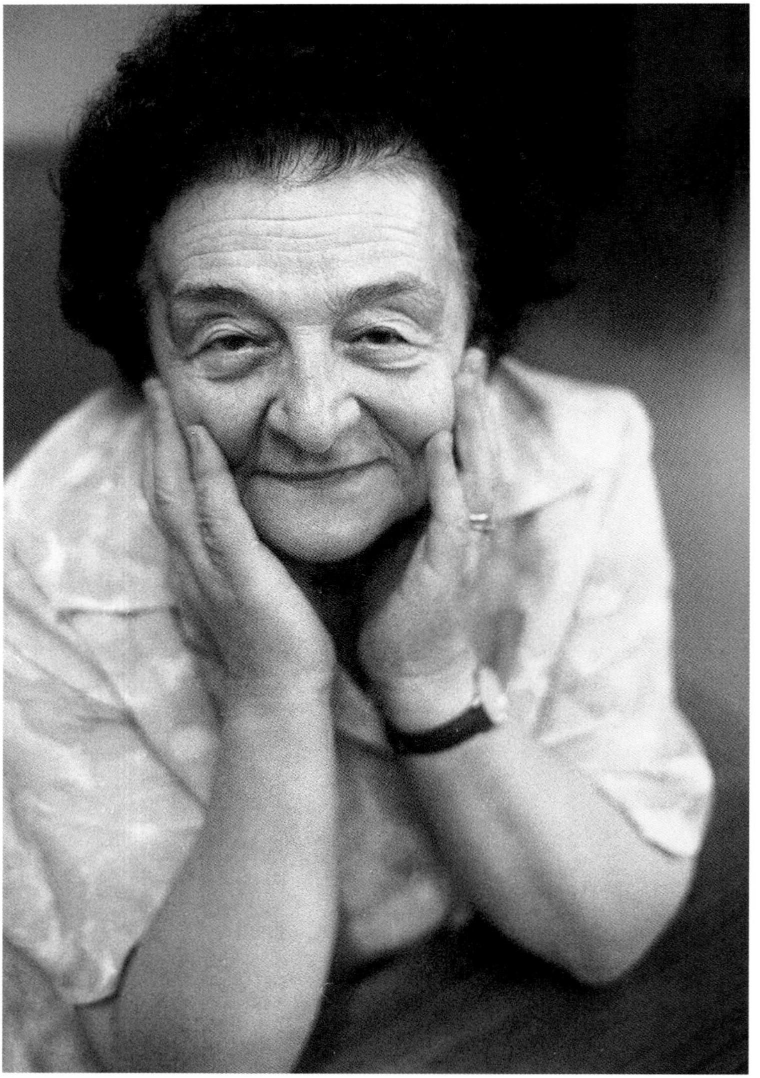

Feiga Kaganskienė. Born 1926

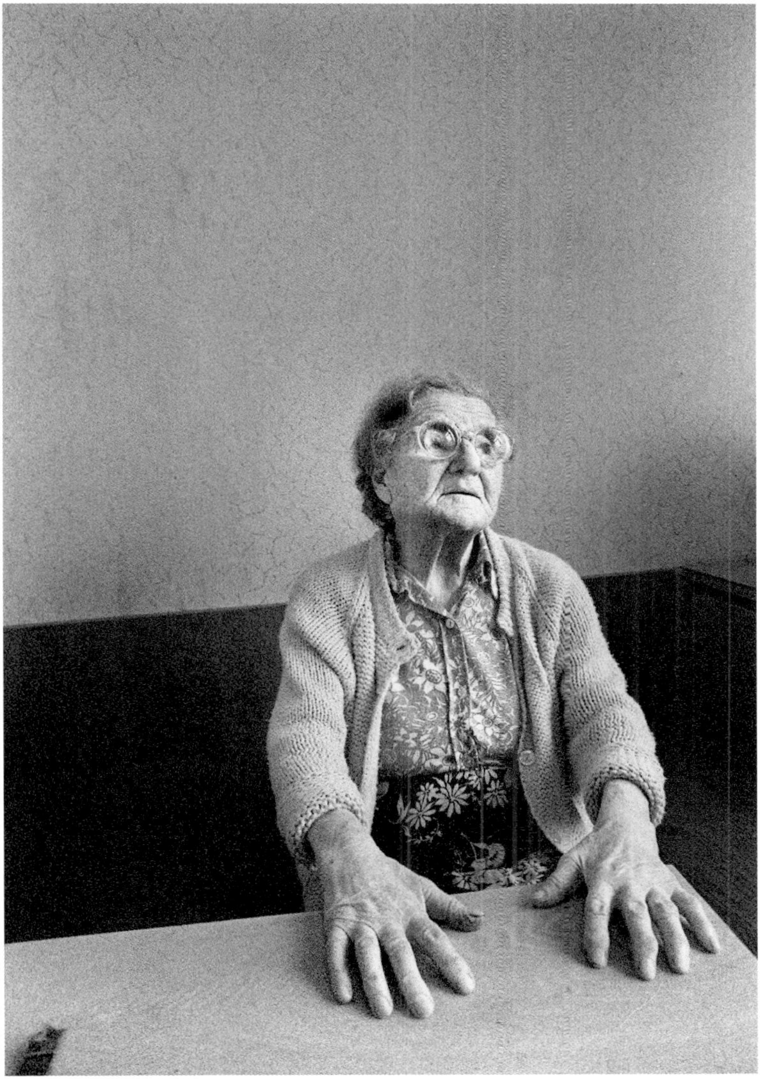

Chana Lisienė. Born 1912

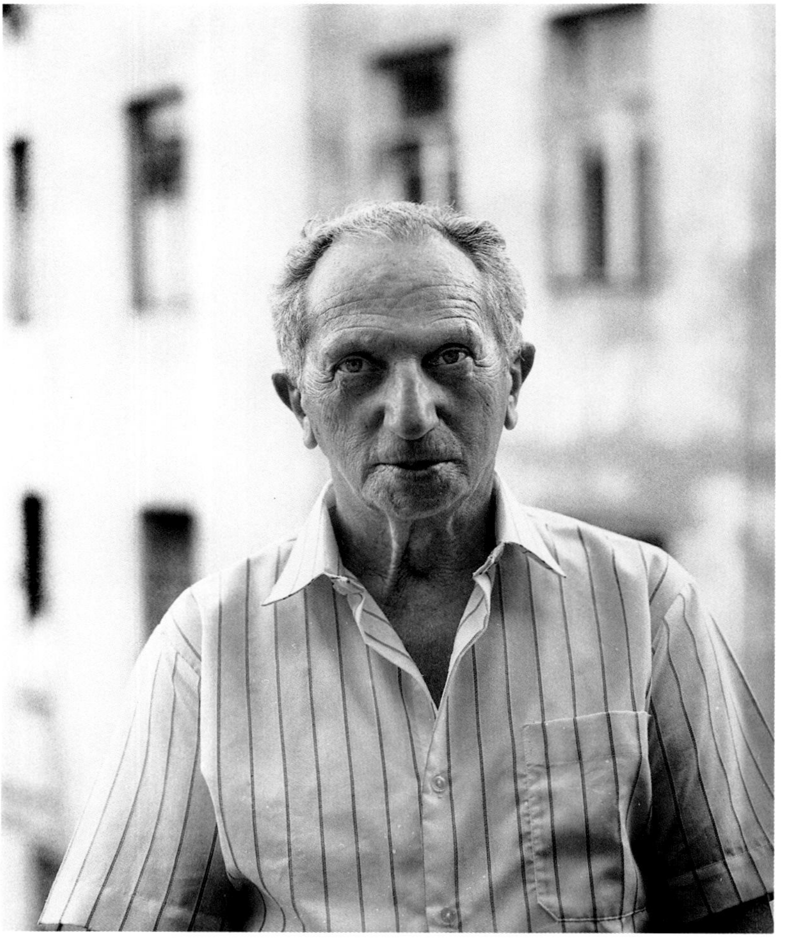

Ziunia Štromas. Born 1920

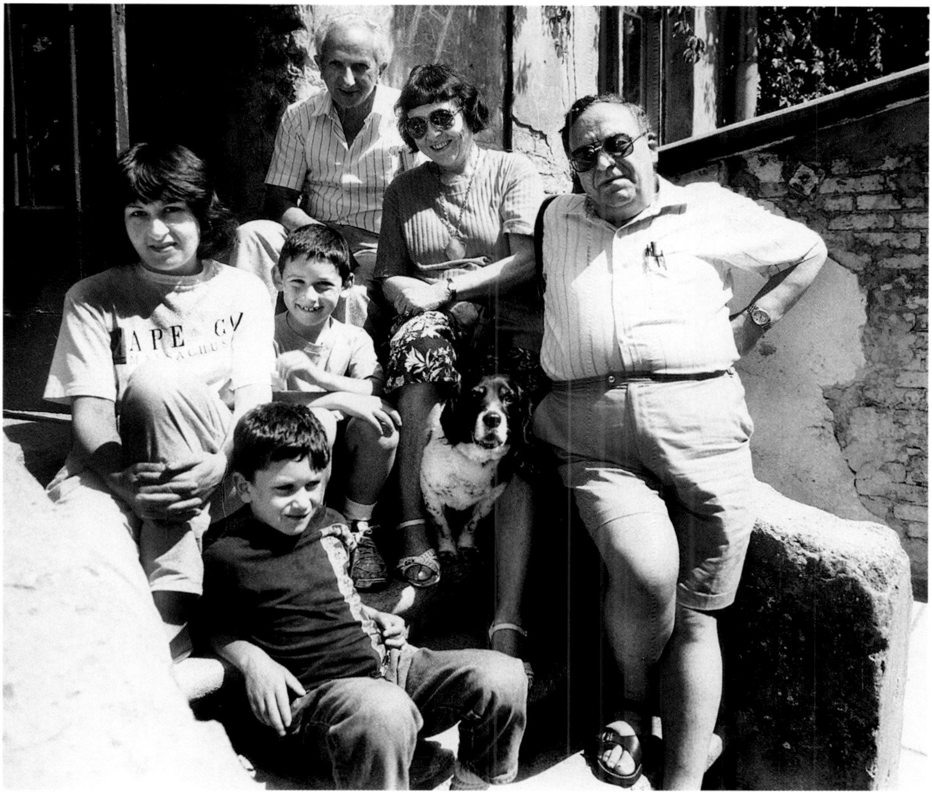

Ziunia Štromas, Irena Veisaitė, Aleksandras Štromas. Born 1932

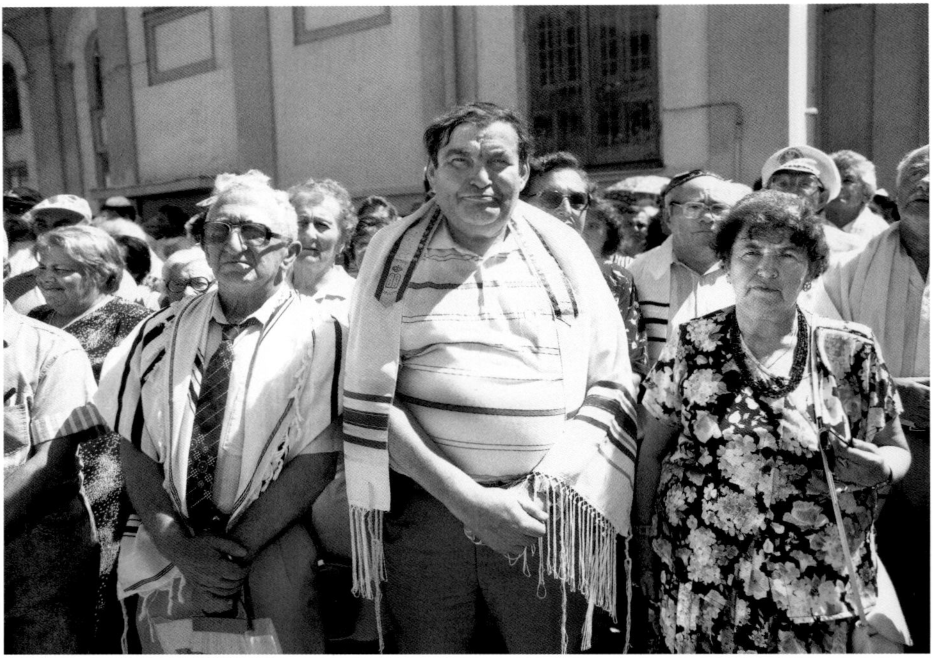

Commemoration meeting to mark the 50th anniversary of the liquidation of the Kaunas ghetto. 1994

INTERVIEWS

August 2016

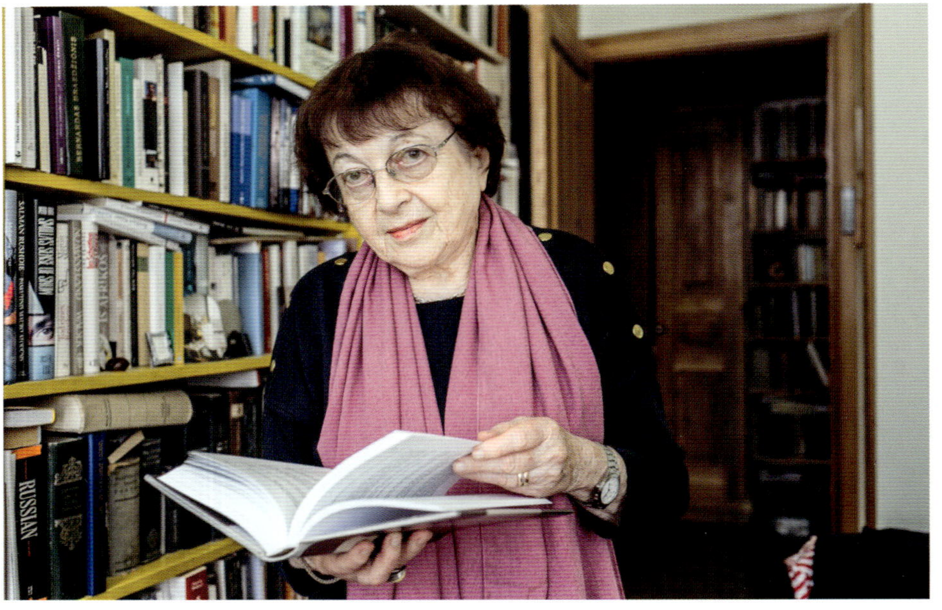

PROFESSOR IRENA VEISAITE

My parents divorced in 1938. Mother was arrested on Thursday, 15th July, 1941. She was 35 years old. She died in prison. During her arrest I was kicked out of a hospital room. The doctor told me to leave, and to bring her clothes from home. The doctor didn't want to allow arresting my mother; he said she was a patient. I stayed in the hospital and helped nurses as there were many wounded people. My mother was watched by a guard, a so called Lithuanian activist, one of those who started riots on the 23rd of June in 1941. That was the beginning of the Holocaust in Lithuania. The guard wasn't there when I spoke to my mother for the very last time. She told me which friends I should go to and stay with. She told me to be independent and subsist according to my means, to live in truth and not to seek vengeance. Later on in life it saved me from hatred.

I was 13, when my maternal grandparents, my sister and I moved to the ghetto. I saw all sorts there. In 1943, our friends gave me fake documents. I ran away, but I didn't hide. I worked at the children's nursery. I was taken care of by the family where I found my "new mother". She was a Lithuanian,

from a famous family. In 1946, she was arrested and sent to Siberia. Following her arrest, her daughters left the house. From that time on, I was looked after by Dr. Browas, who immigrated to America later.
I was eager to study. I graduated from college after 3 years. In 1947, I entered a university, where I took a course in Lithuanian Language and Literature. During my student years in Lithuania, I was constantly approached by the Soviet secret service asking for collaboration. I could not stay in Lithuania any longer and moved to Moscow. Between 1948 and 1953, I studied German Literature at the Moscow University. I achieved excellent results and received a prestigious Lermontov's Grant, but could not receive a first class university diploma, because of my nationality. There was a lot of uncertainty at the time I wanted to go back to Lithuania. Those were the days of the horrifying political persecution and the well-known political case, a so called Doctors' plot was at its height (an accusation of a group of Jewish doctors of conspiring to kill Soviet leaders). In April, the case against the doctors was dropped and I moved to Leningrad to continue my German studies. I completed my Heinrich Heine thesis in 1963. In 1955, I had a baby girl. My daughter lives in England now.

Interview by Anya Stonelake

WHAT DOES THE HOLOCAUST MEAN TO ME?

Sometime ago, Reverend Arunas, the Dean of Bernardine Church asked me: "Irena, what does the Holocaust mean to you?"
This is a very personal question and, having thought about it for several months, I'll try answering it in a personal way. Straight after the end of the war I instinctively avoided remembering. It would have been unbearable. I lost my mother who was only 35 years old. I lost my grandparents, people I knew from my parent's generation and all of my friends. The death is impossible to explain and even harder to justify. Where did so much cruelty suddenly come from? I could not comprehend why I, as a Jew, became a "marked person", humiliated and hunted. I also could not comprehend why this horrific crime – not only against the Jews, but a crime against humanity – was hushed up or distorted in the years, following the end of the war.

The self-sacrifice and kindness of people, which I experienced during those terrible times, probably helped to save me from a complete despair. Engraved in my memory were my mother's last commandments, the meaning of which I was able to comprehend and appreciate only much later in life: live in truth and never seek revenge. I will never forget my rescuers: the dear Bagdonavicius and the Strimaitis families, my "second mother" Stefanija-Ladigiene, Dr Izidorius Rudaitis, Miss Marcele Kubiliute and others. They all risked their own and their children's lives while rescuing mine. I could write a poem about every one of them and today, in Bernardine Church I wish to bow my head low in their memory. Those people not only saved my life, but they helped me to stay away from hatred and anger, and to recover my faith in human kind.
I realised that I could not escape from the horrific memories of the Nazi occupation, however hard I tried. They continue to resurface from my subconscious. For example, I can never go to a communal bath – it reminds me of gas chambers. It always made me incredibly happy if I had enough food to give to my daughter Alina. I neither could, nor can even today, throw away the smallest crust of bread; and if I see any discarded food scraps in the street, I always think that they could save a life of a Holocaust or a Gulag prisoner... I must say that the Holocaust and the Gulag are somehow mixed in my mind. My "second mother" was sent to the Gulag. To this day, I find it difficult to speak calmly about my mother's most cruel death, and about the suffering of Stefanija Ladigiene in Siberia.
Having reached the "honourable" age, I understand that the Holocaust always was and will remain a part of me, that it had a huge effect on my life and the shape of my moral values. I must say that with time my memories are becoming more vivid and resurface from my subconscious more frequently. I am still unable to comprehend how this happened in Europe, in a civilized world, in my native Lithuania.
In answer to Reverend Arunas' question of what the Holocaust meant to me, I could say that now, after 60 years since those terrible events, I am still trying to understand what lessons I have learnt.
I know that I shall never forget those who perished,
I shall always treasure their memory but shall never impose my pain on others. Every person irrespective of nationality or religion forms his or her own relationship with the Holocaust.
I think that my experience of the Holocaust has taught me:
To show sympathy and understanding to others and never to compare depths

of suffering. Everybody experiences their own suffering as the worst;
Never to assume that suffering allows one to claim advantages, and not to project oneself as a victim;
Not to stigmatise anyone with the Star of David or any other national, religious or ethnic symbol with an intention to humiliate;
Never do to others what was done to me;
Never blame a nation for the offences committed by some of its people or its government;
I have learnt that in order to continue living one has to learn to love and forgive.
It is impossible to say everything. I would like to conclude my brief speech with the words of the late sculptor and artist Elena Gaputyte from her preface to a book by Dalia Grinkeviciute, Lithuanians by the Laptev Sea. This book was published in Lithuanian and English and illustrated with photographs of Elena Gaputyte's installations, in which she used white pebbles, candles and lanterns. She said that these were the symbols of peace, everlasting hope and eternal life. I quote Elena's words: "These "burning" installations are a reminder that a man's path is the path of forgiveness and the only path towards life".
I don't know, Reverand Arunas, if I had answered your question. I am not certain that I am able to answer it even for myself…

Professor Irena Veisaite
Vilnius, Bernardinu Church
September 23, 2008

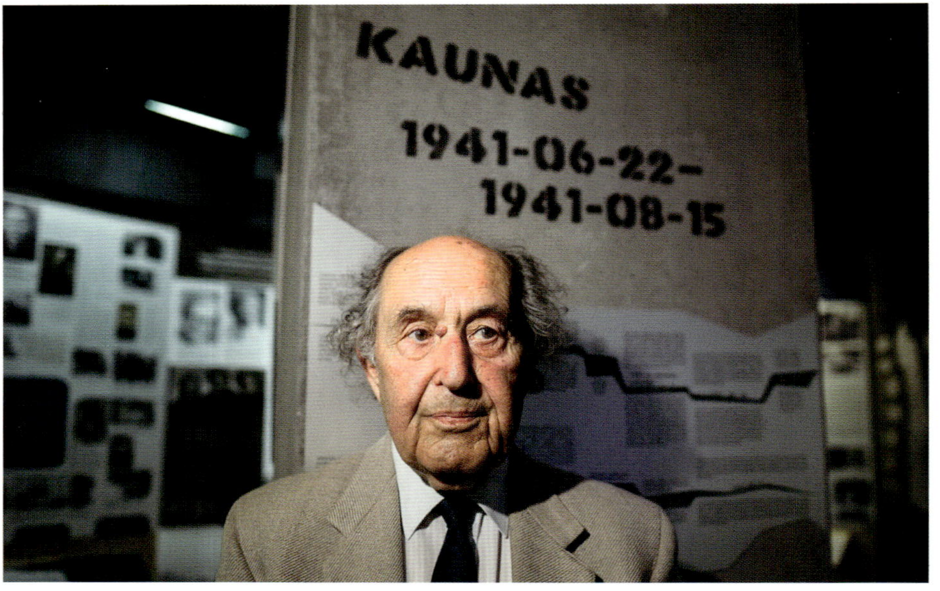

TOBIJAS JAFETAS

I was born two hours before the 1st of April 1930. In Palanga, the war between Russia and Germany began on the night of the 22nd of July 1941, in a place called Nimerzat, the meaning of this name is 'never full'. It was a German territory in Klaipeda region. I became a trefny, i.e. non-kosher. We were all taken into a synagogue. There were no young men, only women and children. We were kept there for three days without any food. Afterwards, we were moved into a camp, located two kilometres away towards Kreitinga. There were six hundred people: small children, old women, teenagers. I was there for eleven days. We cleaned the rooms previously occupied by the Soviet Red Army. I was told by the other kids that I should flee. I ran away back to Kaunas where my mum was at the time. The pogroms began. My cousin's family, aunt Franya and cousin Frankel, helped me to escape. In Kaunas, a ghetto was set up in Vilijampole area; that's where we moved to. Previously, we had a five-bedroom house where we left all the furniture and everything else, and went into the ghetto carrying only a few belongings. In the ghetto, we were cramped into one small room. Before the existence of the ghetto, poor people lived this side of the river. Then, they moved into our houses, and we moved into theirs.

I began training right away. For six months, I was training to become a metal worker. Before long, big things started to happen. Out of 30,000 Jews, one third was split and sent into the 9th fort (the extermination place). Those were the children and older people.
I remained in the ghetto doing various jobs and running errands. Lithuanian, Belorussian, Latvian and Ukrainian voluntary police watched the border. Germans were in small numbers, as most of them were fighting the war. There were about ten of them in charge of a ghetto of approximately 20,000 Jews.
There were several small 'events', when people were gathered to be moved out of the ghetto for the following fabricated reasons: those, who could not work, such as small children, sick and old people were told that they would be moved to a different ghetto. Educated people were told that they would work in the library. In truth, they were taken to the death camps.
My main activity was finding food.
My mother was born in 1893. She had three children. One of them died in 1938. My father was a major trader in English textiles. My aunt on my father's side lived in London, where he and my brother moved. I came to stay with them in London together with my mother and our cousin. We lived in England for six weeks. My cousin graduated from Brighton College, which I attended too during my stay in England. Just before the Second World War began, we returned to Kaunas. Shortly, the Russians occupied Lithuania. My cousin's father was Lithuanian, so when the Germans invaded, my cousin's family was safe.
The 'cleansing' of the children began after three years of the ghetto. One day my mother came back from work, and told me that I should disappear. She organised my escape. Her sister, who was married to a Lithuanian, came to Kaunas to collect me. I escaped through a hole in the fence. I was told that I should become dumb and blind. I was given a new identity in the name of Jonas Vyaikyavichus. At the end of 1944, with this identity document, I was brought to Vilnius. My mother also wanted to escape. In our ghetto house there were no more children left. Sometimes, the mothers were killed together with their infants.
My mother put on her best clothes and set off. She gave all of her valuable belongings to the ghetto guard and made a deal with him to escape. He took the valuables and let her walk off. He then shot her in the back. I don't know where she was buried. Later, the Soviets built a factory on the plot of land where the ghetto was. I was hidden illegally in Vilnius in my aunt's and uncle's three-bedroom apartment. They had two Lithuanian lodgers, one was a po-

liceman and the other was a student. At one point the policemen got married and they had a wedding party in the apartment. I was rolled up in a carpet and hidden under the bed, away from the guests.
When the Soviet army entered Vilnius on the 13th of July 1944, my aunt and I hid in the 17th century Saint Jacob's Cathedral next to the Square (which was named the Lenin Square under the Soviet occupation) and the Conservatoire.
Later, I finished the second year of school and passed the third year's exams over the summer. I finished the fourth, fifth and sixth years in the same boys' school. Then, I completed the Workers and Peasants course, and studied chemistry at the University, where I graduated with honours in 1949.
My wife and I met when I was 25; we had been married for 61 years. We have one daughter who lives in Vilnius, two grandchildren and two great-grandchildren.

Interview by Anya Stonelake

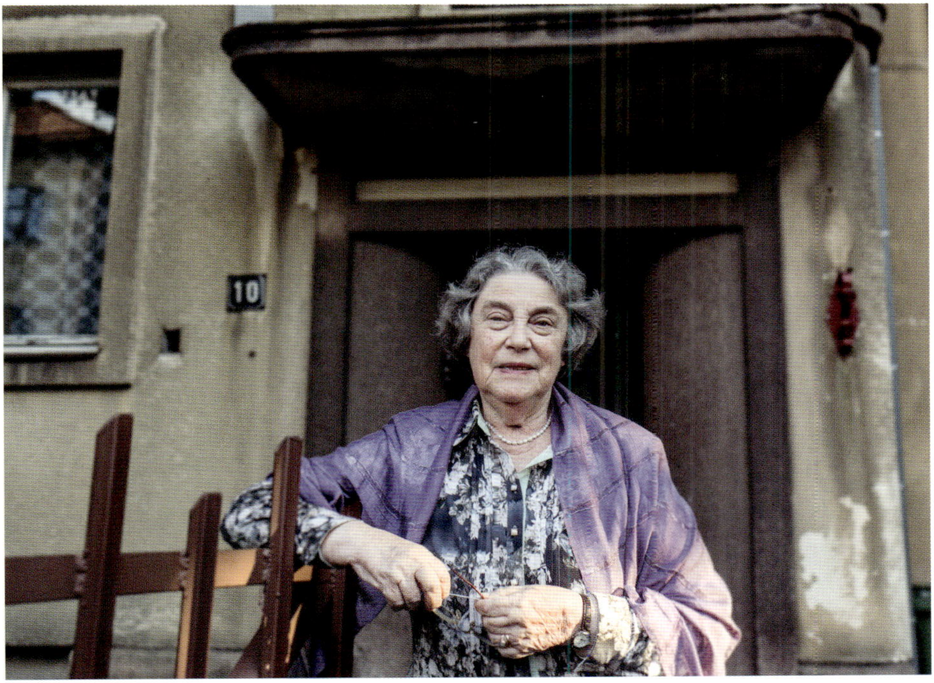

FRUMA VITKINAITĖ

How did the war start for you?

Since we were living in Kaunas, very near to the country's border, it started very suddenly. I remember the first bombings very well, at the end of the day, I was already eight years old. Father said: "Military exercises!" We tried to leave with the Red Army when it turned out that those weren't the "military exercises", and that the Germans were almost here. I remember it all very well. We were unable to get into a train or a truck; we could only find a horse-drawn cart. So we took the cart.

Even now, when I travel down that road to Ukmerge, I can see it all. It's not that I still have nightmares, but I realise that when we passed that church, the bomb had dropped or right there we came under gunfire from two sides of some unexpectedly appeared Lithuanian resistance. Someplace, after we passed Jonava, we stopped to rest in a shed, and there my parents understood that there's no point to run any further, because the Germans were ahead of us now. So we had to return.

Does this mean that Jewish people grasped what German occupation meant? Were there any illusions as to what the Germans would do?

Yes, everybody understood, and there was a complete panic. You see, before the war and even before the Soviet regime, I went to nursery. All of a sudden, one day our nursery teacher spoke of Hitler as if he was some kind of a hero. When I came home, I resentfully told this to my parents, and they decided that I should stop going to nursery straight away. This means that I understood a Hitler threat even then.

Did your parents know about Kaunas pogrom when you were returning back to the town?

Most probably my parents knew about that, because we didn't return to our home. We stayed just outside town with some Jewish friends, where many of those who returned stayed for a few weeks. Finally, when we returned home, my father and my brother were arrested by some activists with white arm bands and taken to the military police office. After three days, they miraculously returned home, which was extremely rare, possibly, because our Lithuanian neighbour, who was in the military, intervened. Following that, of course, frightening times arrived. For the Jewish people the orders were already in place requiring them to wear stars, forbidding walking on pavements or purchasing food. I had light hair and my mother took the star off so that I could go to the smallest possible shops to buy something. Generally, I prefer to speak about what had saved me rather than of things that were frightening to me. You see, at the age of eight I already spoke several languages. By 1941, I finished first year of a Lithuanian school, since some of the Jewish schools became Lithuanian at the time. My father was an engineer at a hosiery factory, where local Germans lived, and where I started to learn German. Next door lived a German boy, who was my friend, and I often visited his home. In our home everyone spoke Yiddish, but sometimes my parents spoke Russian so the children could not understand their conversation. All this knowledge helped me in the future.

How do you remember the move into a ghetto?

You know, by that time the life was so tough that I don't remember the actual move into a ghetto as something terrible. Compared to the previous nine months, when I had to hide, I even remember the ghetto as a place of relative safety, because my parents returned home every evening after working shifts. My grandfather had swapped houses with a Lithuanian woman – his house in Green Hill for a smaller house in Slobodka, which was located by the main gates of the ghetto, on a street, where the shift workers walked in teams to work. All my relatives lived there; in the beginning there were fifteen of us.

What was the life like for a child in the ghetto? Was there anything normal – school, games?

At the start, before 1942, there was an official school. Of course, the standard of teaching was poor, since everyone strived to get a proper job. Everybody tried to get into teams of shift workers, because if you were hard-working you were less likely to get killed. That's why teachers and even doctors worked in these shift teams. Nevertheless, this school protected us, children, from anxiety. Later, the school and the Synagogue, the prayer house to be exact, were closed, but we started to be educated in secret by the rabbi. Of course, not very parent was brave enough to let their children go there. Coming back to what had saved me - my parents tried to always keep me occupied. Soon, it was forbidden to go outside even during the day, and I remember taking the back paths covertly, along the hedges, to get to that rabbi. Something else that had saved me was friendship with the next door kids – two boys and a girl called Goldele. She died, and one of the boys also died in Dachau. I had a responsibility to look after my little cousin, a baby boy called Yankele. These children, especially the boys, had really helped me. I even remember doing some stealing for the baby. I think it was a couple of carrots from some neighbours' vegetable plot. I cooked these carrots just for him, I didn't eat any. We also played games in those boys' courtyard. Their house is still there as it was then, even today. What were those games? The games were about what we saw around us. We pretended that the girls came back from the team shift work, and the boys would search the girls' bags for something eatable. Naturally, we didn't play the same games as before the war.

How you were taken out of the ghetto?

My mother had a relative and a close friend called Rivka, she was a wife of a famous poet, Girsha Osherovich. Once, after New Year's Day at the start of 1942, Rivka vanished. We understood she fled the ghetto. Before the war she worked for a well-known attorney in Kaunas, and was a familiar person in town. She was hidden by two local Russian women in their house; both called Natasha – Natasha Fugalevich and Natasha Egorova – my darling Natashas. Approximately at the same time, my mother thought of another idea to keep me busy and taught me how to knit gloves. People knew that Fruma could knit gloves, they brought me knitting wool, and I made the gloves free of charge. One day, it was already 1943, by that time everyone knew that the children were also in danger; I was lying in my bed and heard a stranger coming in and saying my name. I thought: "Ah, the gloves." It turned out that Rivka asked the Natashas to help me escape from the ghetto as well, and sent a message via a woman from a shift work team. A Jewish ghetto policeman helped me to run away. The policeman put me on his back and was pretending to keep the order in the workers' convoy by shouting: "Order! Order!" in German, and trying to move outside little by little at the same time. People in the convoy realised what was happening, and had surrounded us tightly, like a flow of water, – that's how we got outside the gates. Outside I was told to look for a woman wearing a fashionable at that time phosphorus brooch, and to ask her what time it was. As it happened, it was one of the Natashas herself. The long, round way to her house laid via a hill and the River Neris, I got really scared on the way. I was not frightened by Natasha, I was frightened by the jolly people and their normal life, which was very different to the life I got used to in the last two and a half years in the ghetto. I kept silent all the way, and only when I got inside their house and saw Rivka, I finally started crying.

How did you hide for the next nine months?

At first, I lived with the Natashas and, afterwards, at many other peoples' houses. Moreover, I stayed at the Catholic orphanage on the fake Lithuanian girl's birth certificate in the name of Danute. However, my main hiding spot was at a German lady's house, Helene Holzman. She was married to a Jewish man called Max Holzman. They were artists who moved, as they thought at the time temporarily, to Lithuania. Max was a WWI soldier, Lithuania revealed to him a Jewish cultural realm, which was already extinct and assimilated in Germany. So they stuck here. Max was killed during the first days of German occupation, and Helene stayed with her daughter Gretta, who I call sister today. I probably spent two months with them. After the war, when I found out that nobody from my family survived, I lived with them for many years until I got married.

How did you survive the Soviet offensive?

In July 1944, when the Russians advanced, Natasha Fougalevich took me from the orphanage into their small country house in Kulautuva. All that time, her sister Lida lived there too and supplied us with food. Rivka already moved in there alone with the Rosen family – fifteen Jewish people all together. We lived almost near the front line, but were still in danger because nearby the Germans were retreating, and all of us had to hide in the shed, under a stack of hay at times. The very last time we hid, we hid in the woods. On our side of Neman River the Germans were retreating, on the opposite bank the Russians were attacking. The artillery was firing non-stop. We slept in the woods for three nights. Somehow, a Russian soldier or a resistance fighter was also with us. He built a shield to hide us from view. We even had a cow with us! Suddenly, one morning, we woke up and were told – that's it, there's no more danger. We greeted the Soviet Army in a group of Jewish and Russian people standing at the road junction and giving the soldiers milk and honey. When we ran out of milk, we gave them water to show some hospitality. By the way, that was the 16th Division. There were many high ranking officers, young Jewish men, who managed to evacuate from Kaunas in 1941. They immediately wanted to adopt some of the Jewish orphans including me. At the time, we didn't know what happened to our parents and, of course, Rivka wouldn't allow that.

Interview by Petr Favorov

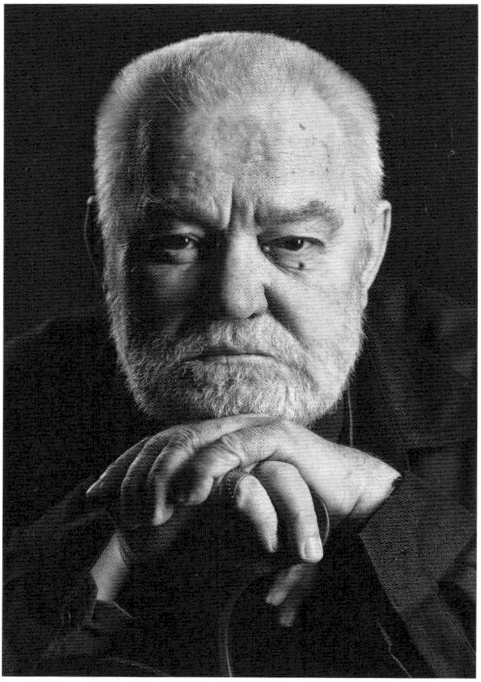

ANTANAS SUTKUS

In 1988, just before Lithuania regained its independence, Lithuanian Jews met in Kaunas to remind the world of their existence. Among them there were a few who happened to survive the massacre in the 9th Fort in Kaunas. The Holocaust in the re-emerging Lithuania was big news to many as the Soviet regime kept rigid silence on the subject. "Only then I've realised how many Jews had been murdered here, in Lithuania. The numbers were shocking – 200,000. During the Soviet times, there was no news or literature on the Holocaust, let alone photography. The truth was suppressed," remembers Antanas Sutkus who took part in the unsanctioned meeting.

I've met the artist at his home studio in Vilnius, every possible space layered with photographs, albums and notes. The cause of our meeting lay in the box beside. In it – a couple of dozen black-and-white portraits, staring directly into my eyes. The inscription on the box "Ghetto" revealed that these were not ordinary people. The content of the box testifies to one of the darkest times in our history.

The series In Memoriam came about very naturally. After some inquiries about the surviving inmates of the Kaunas Ghetto, Antanas Sutkus started visiting them at home.
"I've met one, then another. Started taking pictures. And you know, there was not a single burst of anger or reproach to us, Lithuanians. Though I remember asking one lady, a survivor of the Kaunas Ghetto, about those who took part in those shootings".
"Did Lithuanians shoot people too?"
"Alas, yes," followed an instant answer.
People looking at us from these photographs are people of Lithuania. They are our neighbors: engineers and workers, teachers and artists. The series was created in 1988 – 1997; hence, most of the characters already became a part of history. Time had been relentless to the last survivors of ghetto atrocities. Now only a few witnesses remain alive.

Antanas Sutkus is undoubtedly a photographic connoisseur of Lithuanian people. I ask him what in the eye of a photographer makes these people different from the others. "I've instantly noticed that their faces are different. Their souls show on the faces - the souls of people who had suffered extensively. And there was warmth. They talked with me, posed before my camera but there was not a single hint about the men who shot Jews. And accordingly, I did not want to rub salt into their wounds, to raise political or Holocaust issues, to disturb them before the camera. I simply took pictures of people who retained their dignity in the perils of the Holocaust. This is my maxim that I am faithful to at all times – to show humanity, stamina and national character."
Sutkus sees the Holocaust as the heaviest form of Nazi metastases. Thus, there cannot be too much talking about the Holocaust, as well as support and heed for its survivors. "When a young lady was asked by a journalist in a street what is the Holocaust, she hesitated for a moment and said that maybe it is some wallpaper glue."
"Anti-Semitism does not have a nationality. It springs into being where darkness prevails. Therefore now, when Europe is undergoing a surge in immigration, wars and acts of terror, it is the right time to remember the lessons of the Holocaust."

Interview by Artūras Morozovas

BIOGRAPHIES

Antanas Sutkus (born 1939) bought his first camera as a child, having not earned enough to buy a bicycle when digging peat with his mother. He later became a photojournalist and, since 1968, has worked as an independent photographer. He has also helped Lithuanian photographers gain international recognition as co-founder and President of the Photography Art Society of Lithuania, which championed photography as an art form. His humanistic approach comes to the fore in both his images of children and old people. Filled with romance, beauty and sadness, they move beyond photographic realism like stills from an unmade film. His stated aim is 'to make an attempt at drawing a psychological portrait of contemporary man'. Beyond recording events, Sutkus' keen eye finds history in human faces 'One has to love people in order to take pictures of them.' His black and white portraits manage to avoid sentimentality but have great pathos.
In 2001-02, Sutkus won the Erna & Victor Hasselblad Foundation Grant, Sweden, for 'Documentation and Conservation of Antanas Sutkus' Archive of Photographs'. In 2015 he has been granted the honourable state award of France – the order of art and literature for the dissemination of French culture.

Arturas Morozovas (born 1984) belongs to a young generation of photojournalists in Lithuania. He is working actively since 2007 and documenting sensitive social topics, worldwide stories such as war in Ukraine, Migrant crisis in Europe. His photographies recently were published in such well-known media outlets as "The Guardian", "Der Spiegel", "NyTimes", "Le Nouvel Observateur", "Taz", etc. Arturas received multiple international and Lithuanian awards for his work. His photographs were exhibited in Belgium, Italy, Lithuania, Russia, Georgia, Ukraine.

Leonidas Donskis is a Lithuanian philosopher, historian of ideas, and writer. He is a former member of the European Parliament (2009–2014). Donskis has written and edited over fifty books, seventeen of them in English. He combines political theory, history of ideas, philosophy of culture, philosophy of literature, and essayistic style. Among other books, he is co-author (together with Zygmunt Bauman) of Liquid Evil: Living with TINA (2016) and Moral Blindness: The Loss of Sensitivity in Liquid Modernity (2013), and the author of The Unbearable Lightness of Change: Essays on Two Europes (2015); Fifty Letters from the Troubled Modern World: A Philosophical-Political Diary, 2009–2012 (2013), Modernity in Crisis: A Dialogue on the Culture of Belonging (2011), Troubled Identity and the Modern World (2009), Power and Imagination: Studies in Politics and Literature (2008), and Forms of Hatred: The Troubled Imagination in Modern Philosophy and Literature (2003). His works originally written in Lithuanian and English have been translated into Brazilian Portuguese, Danish, Estonian, Finnish, Georgian, German, Hungarian, Italian, Korean, Polish, Portuguese, Romanian, Russian, Spanish, Swedish, Turkish, and

Ukrainian. He is also the author of several books of aphorisms published in Canada, Italy, and Lithuania. He is Professor of Politics and Director of the Academia cum Laude (Honors Programme) at Vytautas Magnus University, Kaunas, Lithuania. Donskis holds an Honorary Degree of Doctor of Letters from the University of Bradford, UK (2011), and an Honorary Degree of Doctor Honoris Causa from Valahia University in Târgovişte, Romania (2014). Leonidas Donskis is also the Honorary Consul of Finland in Kaunas, Lithuania.

Kamilė Rupeikaitė is a Deputy Director for Research at the Vilna Gaon Jewish State Mueseum in Vilnius, Lithuania. The first Jewish museum was established in Vilnius in 1913.Their activities were interrupted with the outbreak of WWI. In 1919, noted Jewish writer Sholom Zanvil Rapoport (Sh. An-sky) revived the society. On the eve of WWII, the Museum housed over 3000 objects and 6000 books, many valuable documents including original texts of the privileges granted to Jews by the Grand Dukes the late Middle Ages. In September 1941, the Nazis established the Vilnius and Kaunas divisions of the Alfred Rosenberg Headquarters. The goal of these units was to collect Lithuania's Jewish artistic and cultural valuables, which amounted to the plundering and destruction of a large portion of Lithuanian Jewry's cultural heritage. The libraries and museums were ransacked. A group of inmates from the Vilnius ghetto were forced to assist the Rosenberg Headquarters in this infamous work. Those Jewish intellectuals risked their lives to save the valuable items. In the ghetto, special hiding places were prepared to store the rescued items.

In the summer of 1944, a Jewish museum, the only one in the Soviet Union, was established in Vilnius. Jewish survivors who returned to the city founded the museum shortly after the withdrawal of Nazi troops. Apart from collecting and preserving the Jewish cultural heritage, they also listed the addresses of returning Jewish survivors. The museum became the spiritual and cultural center for Vilnius Jews where all current problems facing the community were discussed. Surviving Jewish cultural treasures were brought to this location from numerous hiding places.

Throughout the Soviet period, the existence of a Jewish museum or any Jewish institution in Soviet Lithuania was impossible. Only the Paneriai and Kaunas 9th Fort memorials made vague reference to the Jews, as victims of the Holocaust. Jewish history and heritage seemed doomed to total obliteration.

The situation suddenly changed with the Perestroyka reforms in the late 1980s. The Government of Soviet Lithuania passed Resolution permitting the re-opening of the Jewish Museum after 50 years of non-existence. In 1989 the M.K. Čiurlionis Art Gallery in Kaunas donated the surviving objects it had in storage. These treasures became the basis for the Jewish Museum's collection. In 1997,on the 200th anniversary of the death of renowned Torah scholar the Gaon of Vilna, the museum was renamed the Vilna Gaon State Jewish Museum.

In Memoriam Album

First edition of 1600 copies
Published in 2016 by
White Space Gallery
London, UK
info@whitespacegallery.co.uk
www.whitespacegallery.co.uk

Printed by Keuruun Laatupaino Oy, Finland